To

From

Message

Promises from God for Powerful Living

© 2006 Christian Art Gifts, RSA
Christian Art Gifts Inc., IL, USA

Designed by Christian Art Gifts
Compiled by Lynette Douglas

Scripture quotations are taken from the *Holy Bible,* New International Version®. NIV®. Copyright © 1973, 1978, 1984 by International Bible Society. Used by permission of Zondervan Publishing House. All rights reserved.

Scripture quotations are taken from the *Holy Bible,* King James Version. Copyright © 1962 by The Zondervan Corporation. Used by permission. All rights reserved.

Scripture quotations are taken from the *Holy Bible,* New King James Version. Copyright © 1979, 1980, 1982 by Thomas Nelson Publishers, Inc. Used by permission. All rights reserved.

Scripture quotations are taken from the *Holy Bible,* English Standard Version. Copyright © 2001 by Crossway Bibles, a division of Good News Publishers. Used by permission. All rights reserved.

ISBN 1-86920-537-5

© All rights reserved. No part of this book may be reproduced in any form without permission in writing from the publisher, except in the case of brief quotations embodied in critical articles or reviews.

Printed in China

06 07 08 09 10 11 12 13 14 15 – 10 9 8 7 6 5 4 3 2 1

Promises from God for
Powerful Living

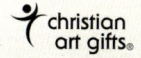

christian art gifts

Contents

Introduction	7
Abiding in Christ	8
Blessings	12
Christian Character	16
Closeness to God	20
Contentment	24
Courage	28
Discipleship	32
Faith	36
Finances	40
Forgiveness	44
Freedom	48
God's Care	52
God's Will	56
Goodness	60
Grace	64
Guidance	68
Heaven	72
Holiness	76
Inheritance	80
Jesus Christ	84
The Kingdom of God	88

Life	92
Miracles	96
Perseverance	100
Growth	104
Praise and Worship	108
Prayer	112
Priorities	116
Rest	120
Self-worth	124
Strength	128
Success	132
Thankfulness	136
Time	140
Wisdom	144
Womanhood	148
Work	152

Introduction

He is not weak in dealing with you, but is powerful among you. For to be sure, he was crucified in weakness, yet he lives by God's power. Likewise, we are weak in him, yet by God's power we will live with him to serve you.

2 Corinthians 13:3-4 NIV

In the heart of every person there is a desire to live a passionate and powerful life. Jesus came to earth and died on the cross so that we may have that life, and experience it to the full. All you have to do to live abundantly is to give yourself, your plans and your problems to the great Problem-solver.

Experience the pure joy of discipleship and passionate living as you daily grow into the likeness of Christ by walking with your Savior and getting to know Him intimately. By doing this the holy characteristics of God will be revealed through you in love, honesty, selflessness and integrity.

When you submit your whole life to God in obedience, your faith will come alive and you will be united with the greatest Source of power and passion. Decide today to do everything you do with passion and enthusiasm, to the glory of God.

ABIDING IN CHRIST

Your love is ever before me, and I walk continually in Your truth.

Psalm 26:3 NIV

God has granted you a wonderful privilege. He has called you to share in the life of Jesus Christ. When the full meaning of this divine gift dawns on you, the implications are almost too great to envision.

To share in the life of Jesus Christ implies unlimited possibilities, but also great responsibilities. Your understanding of God deepens, your vision of what you can be expands and you become intensely aware of the presence of Christ.

Intimacy with the Master requires that the quality of your life be an expression of your faith. The characteristics of God must be reflected in your life through love, honesty, unselfishness and purity.

Christ offers Himself to you so that you can share in His life and share your life with Him. When you walk in this glorious truth, you will experience Jesus Christ's strength and joy in your life.

Experiencing the Presence of Christ

"I am the vine; you are the branches. If a man remains in me and I in him, he will bear much fruit; apart from me you can do nothing."

John 15:5 NIV

"If anyone does not abide in me, he is cast out as a branch and is withered; and they gather them and throw them into the fire, and they are burned. If you abide in me, and my words abide in you, you will ask what you desire, and it shall be done for you."

John 15:6-7 NKJV

To the Jews who had believed him, Jesus said, "If you hold to my teaching, you are really my disciples."

John 8:31 NIV

"Truly, truly, I say to you, if anyone keeps my word, he will never see death."

John 8:51 ESV

"As the Father hath loved me, so have I loved you: continue ye in my love."

John 15:9 KJV

Promises from God for Powerful Living

"If you love me, you will obey what I command. And I will ask the Father, and he will give you another Counselor to be with you forever – the Spirit of truth. The world cannot accept him, because it neither sees him nor knows him. But you know him, for he lives with you and will be in you."

John 14:15-17 NIV

"In that day you will know that I am in my Father, and you in me, and I in you. Whoever has my commandments and keeps them, he it is who loves me. And he who loves me will be loved by my Father, and I will love him and manifest myself to him."

John 14:20-21 ESV

Jesus answered him, "If anyone loves me, he will keep my word, and my Father will love him, and we will come to him and make our home with him."

John 14:23 ESV

The Spirit Himself bears witness with our spirit that we are children of God.

Romans 8:16 NKJV

But as many as received him, to them gave he power to become the sons of God.

John 1:12 KJV

Abiding in Christ

You, however, are controlled not by the sinful nature but by the Spirit, if the Spirit of God lives in you. And if anyone does not have the Spirit of Christ, he does not belong to Christ.

Romans 8:9 NIV

Don't you know that you yourselves are God's temple and that God's Spirit lives in you?

1 Corinthians 3:16 NIV

Because you are sons, God has sent the Spirit of his Son into our hearts, crying, "Abba! Father!"

Galatians 4:6 ESV

We proclaim to you what we have seen and heard, so that you also may have fellowship with us. And our fellowship is with the Father and with his Son, Jesus Christ.

1 John 1:3 NIV

Whoever keeps His word, truly the love of God is perfected in him. By this we know that we are in Him. He who says he abides in Him ought himself also to walk just as He walked.

1 John 2:5-6, NKJV

BLESSINGS

"Blessed are the pure in heart: for they shall see God."

Matthew 5:8 KJV

God made a special promise to Abraham when He commanded him to take the path of faith and go to the Promised Land. God kept His promise. Abraham was abundantly blessed in temporary things, but the spiritual blessings of his walk of faith could not be measured. He could never have dreamed that the benefits from God's immense treasure-house would be so great.

God's blessing also came through the faithful Abraham to all he came into contact with. As a servant of God, he was a blessing wherever he went. The blessing which God gives us must not be kept to ourselves. As we pray for others God will use us as channels through which His blessing can flow to the world, for His honor and glory.

By revealing the nature of Christ in our lives; by appreciating and praising other people; by encouraging our fellowmen and praying for them, we can be a rich blessing to the greater glory of God in His world.

BOUNTIFUL BLESSINGS

The LORD bless thee, and keep thee: The LORD make his face shine upon thee, and be gracious unto thee: The LORD lift up his countenance upon thee, and give thee peace.

Numbers 6:24-26 KJV

May you be blessed by the LORD, the Maker of heaven and earth.

Psalm 115:15 NIV

Now therefore may it please you to bless the house of your servant, so that it may continue forever before you. For you, O Lord God, have spoken, and with your blessing shall the house of your servant be blessed forever.

2 Samuel 7:29 ESV

Blessed is she who has believed that what the Lord has said to her will be accomplished.

Luke 1:45 NIV

Bless, Lord, his substance, and accept the work of his hands.

Deuteronomy 33:11 KJV

Promises from God for Powerful Living

He replied, "Blessed rather are those who hear the word of God and obey it."

Luke 11:28 NIV

O taste and see that the LORD is good: blessed is the man that trusteth in him.

Psalm 34:8 KJV

Then Jesus told him, "Because you have seen me, you have believed; blessed are those who have not seen and yet have believed."

John 20:29 NIV

Blessed are the people who know the festal shout, who walk, O LORD, in the light of your face.

Psalm 89:15 ESV

"Blessed are those who hunger and thirst for righteousness, for they will be filled."

Matthew 5:6 NIV

"Blessed are the peacemakers, for they will be called sons of God."

Matthew 5:9 NIV

Blessed are all who fear the LORD, who walk in his ways.

Psalm 128:1 NIV

Blessings

Blessed is the man who walks not in the counsel of the wicked, nor stands in the way of sinners, nor sits in the seat of scoffers; but his delight is in the law of the Lord, and on his law he meditates day and night. He is like a tree planted by streams of water that yields its fruit in its season, and its leaf does not wither. In all that he does, he prospers.

Psalm 1:1-3 ESV

All these blessings shall come upon you and overtake you, because you obey the voice of the Lord your God.

Deuteronomy 28:2 NKJV

Blessed be the God and Father of our Lord Jesus Christ, who has blessed us in Christ with every spiritual blessing in the heavenly places.

Ephesians 1:3 ESV

But blessed is the man who trusts in the Lord, whose confidence is in him.

Jeremiah 17:7 NIV

Christian Character

But just as he who called you is holy, so be holy in all you do; for it is written: "Be holy, because I am holy."
1 Peter 1:15-16 NIV

Every Christian should strive to base his life on the pattern of Christ's life. This pattern will vary according to our personalities, but the all-embracing desire should be to become more like Christ.

The acceptance of the lordship of Christ is the beginning of a new and enriching life. He becomes your pattern and your goal. Of course it is impossible to perfect this pattern by yourself, nor can you reach this goal through your own efforts.

When you accept Christ as the Lord of your life, He will give you His Holy Spirit. When you submit your whole life to Him in obedience, your faith comes alive and you are united with Him.

From this unity a Christlike character develops; a humble character where there is no place for false pride. Holiness is the product of fellowship with the Master.

Becoming like Christ

The fruit of the Spirit is love, joy, peace, patience, kindness, goodness, faithfulness, gentleness and self-control; against such things there is no law.

Galatians 5:22-23 ESV

Make every effort to add to your faith goodness; and to goodness, knowledge; and to knowledge, self-control; and to self-control, perseverance; and to perseverance, godliness; and to godliness, brotherly kindness; and to brotherly kindness, love.

2 Peter 1:5-7 NIV

Let the peace of Christ rule in your hearts, to which indeed you were called in one body. And be thankful.

Colossians 3:15 ESV

Put off your old self, which belongs to your former manner of life and is corrupt through deceitful desires, and be renewed in the spirit of your minds, and put on the new self, created after the likeness of God in true righteousness and holiness.

Ephesians 4:22-24 ESV

Promises from God for Powerful Living

Therefore, as God's chosen people, holy and dearly loved, clothe yourselves with compassion, kindness, humility, gentleness and patience. Bear with each other and forgive whatever grievances you may have against one another. Forgive as the Lord forgave you. And over all these virtues put on love, which binds them all together in perfect unity.

Colossians 3:12-14 NIV

Therefore be imitators of God as dear children. And walk in love, as Christ also has loved us and given Himself for us, an offering and a sacrifice to God for a sweet-smelling aroma.

Ephesians 5:1-2 NKJV

He hath shewed thee, O man, what is good; and what doth the LORD require of thee, but to do justly, and to love mercy, and to walk humbly with thy God?

Micah 6:8 KJV

With this in mind, we constantly pray for you, that our God may count you worthy of his calling, and that by his power he may fulfill every good purpose of yours and every act prompted by your faith.

2 Thessalonians 1:11 NIV

Christian Character

And this is my prayer: that your love may abound more and more in knowledge and depth of insight, so that you may be able to discern what is best and may be pure and blameless until the day of Christ, filled with the fruit of righteousness that comes through Jesus Christ – to the glory and praise of God.

Philippians 1:9-11 NIV

God made him who had no sin to be sin for us, so that in him we might become the righteousness of God.

2 Corinthians 5:21 NIV

Finally, all of you, live in harmony with one another; be sympathetic, love as brothers, be compassionate and humble. Do not repay evil with evil or insult with insult, but with blessing, because to this you were called so that you may inherit a blessing.

1 Peter 3:8-9 NIV

For you know that we dealt with each of you as a father deals with his own children, encouraging, comforting and urging you to live lives worthy of God, who calls you into his kingdom and glory.

1 Thessalonians 2:11-12 NIV

CLOSENESS TO GOD

God looks down from heaven on the children of man to see if there are any who understand, who seek after God.

Psalm 53:2 ESV

Praise God because He is with you right now. Humbly ask Him to lead you on His path of righteousness. David realized that it was both wonderful and fearful to know that God is always everywhere.

One can never escape His presence. But in our human weakness, we attempt to do so. Possibly because of our guilty consciences or because we are reluctant to follow through on something that He has asked of us. Like Jonah, we try to flee from God, but no one can escape from the omnipresence of God.

Even if we flee to the realms of the dead in Sheol, He will still be there. There is no dark corner in life that the light of God's presence cannot penetrate. Whatever the consequences of our sins might be, nothing can separate us from the love God has for us.

Forever in God's Presence

Draw near to God, and he will draw near to you.

James 4:8 ESV

"Call to me and I will answer you, and will tell you great and hidden things you have not known."

Jeremiah 33:3 ESV

One thing I ask of the Lord, this is what I seek: that I may dwell in the house of the Lord all the days of my life, to gaze upon the beauty of the Lord and to seek him in his temple.

Psalm 27:4 NIV

Blessed are those you choose and bring near to live in your courts! We are filled with the good things of your house, of your holy temple.

Psalm 65:4 NIV

It is good for me to draw near to God; I have put my trust in the Lord God, that I may declare all Your works.

Psalm 73:28 NKJV

My heart says of you, "Seek his face!" Your face, Lord, I will seek.

Psalm 27:8 NIV

Let us draw near with a true heart in full assurance of faith, with our hearts sprinkled clean from an evil conscience and our bodies washed with pure water.

Hebrews 10:22 ESV

Seek the Lord while he may be found; call on him while he is near.

Isaiah 55:6 NIV

Sow to yourselves in righteousness, reap in mercy; break up your fallow ground: for it is time to seek the Lord, till he come and rain righteousness upon you.

Hosea 10:12 KJV

Then you will call upon me and come and pray to me, and I will listen to you. You will seek me and find me when you seek me with all your heart.

Jeremiah 29:12-13 NIV

God did this so that men would seek him and perhaps reach out for him and find him, though he is not far from each one of us.

Acts 17:27 NIV

Closeness to God

If from thence thou shalt seek the Lord thy God, thou shalt find him, if thou seek him with all thy heart and with all thy soul.

Deuteronomy 4:29 KJV

O God, you are my God; earnestly I seek you; my soul thirsts for you, my flesh faints for you, as in a dry and weary land where there is no water.

Psalm 63:1 ESV

As a deer pants for flowing streams, so pants my soul for you, O God. My soul thirsts for God, for the living God. When shall I come and appear before God?

Psalm 42:1-2 ESV

My soul yearns for you in the night; in the morning my spirit longs for you. When your judgments come upon the earth, the people of the world learn righteousness.

Isaiah 26:9 NIV

God has said, "Never will I leave you; never will I forsake you." So we say with confidence, "The Lord is my helper; I will not be afraid. What can man do to me?"

Hebrews 13:5-6 NIV

CONTENTMENT

My soul will be satisfied as with the richest of foods; with singing lips my mouth will praise you.

Psalm 63:5 NIV

At some time or another everybody longs for peace of mind and inner tranquility. The insecurities of life: sickness, death, dangers and unrest create a deep-seated uncertainty. The list is endless, yet the results are the same: unknown pressure and lack of confidence that border on despair.

Many of those who suffer seek professional help, while others give in to despair and live in a void of worthlessness.

The only proven way to handle the pressures and tensions of life is through faith which is steadfastly founded in the living Christ. You need to experience unity with Him on an ongoing basis. Hold on to Him, talk to Him, regardless of how desperate your situation might be, trust that He is always with you.

Completely Content in Christ

I am not saying this because I am in need, for I have learned to be content whatever the circumstances. I know what it is to be in need, and I know what it is to have plenty. I have learned the secret of being content in any and every situation, whether well fed or hungry, whether living in plenty or in want.

Philippians 4:11-12 NIV

Godliness with contentment is great gain. For we brought nothing into the world, and we can take nothing out of it. But if we have food and clothing, we will be content with that.

1 Timothy 6:6-8 NIV

All the days of the afflicted are evil: but he that is of a merry heart hath a continual feast.

Proverbs 15:15 KJV

Better what the eye sees than the roving of the appetite. This too is meaningless, a chasing after the wind.

Ecclesiastes 6:9 NIV

Promises from God for Powerful Living

Let not your heart envy sinners, but continue in the fear of the Lord all the day. Surely there is a future, and your hope will not be cut off.

Proverbs 23:17-18 esv

Trust in the Lord, and do good; dwell in the land and befriend faithfulness. Delight yourself in the Lord, and he will give you the desires of your heart.

Psalm 37:3-4 esv

The Lord knows the days of the upright, and their inheritance shall be forever. They shall not be ashamed in the evil time, and in the days of famine they shall be satisfied.

Psalm 37:18-19 nkjv

I was young and now I am old, yet I have never seen the righteous forsaken or their children begging bread. They are always generous and lend freely; their children will be blessed.

Psalm 37:25-26 niv

You shall eat and be full, and you shall bless the Lord your God for the good land he has given you.

Deuteronomy 8:10 esv

Contentment

There is nothing better for a man, than that he should eat and drink, and that he should make his soul enjoy good in his labour. This also I saw, that it was from the hand of God.

Ecclesiastes 2:24 KJV

"Come to Me, all you who labor and are heavy laden, and I will give you rest. Take My yoke upon you and learn from Me, for I am gentle and lowly in heart, and you will find rest for your souls. For My yoke is easy and My burden is light."

Matthew 11:28-30 NKJV

Do not be anxious about anything, but in everything, by prayer and petition, with thanksgiving, present your requests to God. And the peace of God, which transcends all understanding, will guard your hearts and your minds in Christ Jesus.

Philippians 4:6-7 NIV

My God shall supply all your need according to His riches in glory by Christ Jesus.

Philippians 4:19 NKJV

COURAGE

The wicked man flees though no one pursues, but the righteous are as bold as a lion.

Proverbs 28:1 NIV

Sometimes when we face the unknown fear tends to overwhelm us. When we try to handle the unknown ourselves, we are robbed of our self-confidence. Many great plans miscarry and never reach fruition because people lack the courage to take action or the perseverance to see them through.

Even your work for the Lord can be handicapped by paralyzing fear. Remember, you will not achieve anything of permanent worth unless you tackle it in God's strength and do it to His honor and glory.

Things of worth are usually achieved only through effort and exertion and perseverance. You will come across stumbling blocks and you will want to give up. But it is important to always make Jesus Christ a partner in your dreams, plans and goals. The assurance that He will lovingly guide you will not let fear paralyze you.

Courageous in the Lord

"Have I not commanded you? Be strong and courageous. Do not be terrified; do not be discouraged, for the Lord your God will be with you wherever you go."

Joshua 1:9 NIV

Wait on the Lord; be of good courage, and He shall strengthen your heart; wait, I say, on the Lord!

Psalm 27:14 NKJV

"I have told you these things, so that in me you may have peace. In this world you will have trouble. But take heart! I have overcome the world."

John 16:33 NIV

Though an host should encamp against me, my heart shall not fear: though war should rise against me, in this will I be confident. One thing have I desired of the Lord, that will I seek after; that I may dwell in the house of the Lord all the days of my life, to behold the beauty of the Lord, and to enquire in his temple.

Psalm 27:3-4 KJV

Only let your manner of life be worthy of the gospel of Christ, so that whether I come and see you or am absent, I may hear of you that you are standing firm in one spirit, with one mind striving side by side for the faith of the gospel, and not frightened in anything by your opponents. This is a clear sign to them of their destruction, but of your salvation, and that from God.

Philippians 1:27-28 ESV

God is our refuge and strength, a very present help in trouble. Therefore we will not fear though the earth gives way, though the mountains be moved into the heart of the sea.

Psalm 46:1-2 ESV

Let us therefore come boldly to the throne of grace, that we may obtain mercy and find grace to help in time of need.

Hebrews 4:16 NKJV

What, then, shall we say in response to this? If God is for us, who can be against us? He who did not spare his own Son, but gave him up for us all – how will he not also, along with him, graciously give us all things?

Romans 8:31-32 NIV

Courage

The Lord also will be a refuge for the oppressed, a refuge in times of trouble.

Psalm 9:9 KJV

So we can confidently say, "The Lord is my helper; I will not fear; what can man do to me?"

Hebrews 13:6 ESV

"Fear thou not; for I am with thee: be not dismayed; for I am thy God: I will strengthen thee; yea, I will help thee; yea, I will uphold thee with the right hand of my righteousness."

Isaiah 41:10 KJV

But now, this is what the Lord says – he who created you, O Jacob, he who formed you, O Israel: "Fear not, for I have redeemed you; I have summoned you by name; you are mine. When you pass through the waters, I will be with you; and when you pass through the rivers, they will not sweep over you. When you walk through the fire, you will not be burned; the flames will not set you ablaze."

Isaiah 43:1-2 NIV

Discipleship

The disciples went and did as Jesus had instructed them.

Matthew 21:6 NIV

How far you have progressed on the Christian path since your conversion? Discipleship implies growing trust, increasing love and unconditional obedience to the Master who keeps your faith strong and meaningful.

Be assured that He will lead you in ever more wonderful ways on the path ahead. Discipleship means oneness with the Lord and as your love for Him inspires you to greater obedience, His presence in your heart will become an ever greater reality in your life.

Discipleship implies continuous growth in Christ until He becomes the greatest motivating force in your life. Then you will discover that you can do nothing without Him, but that with Him you are able to accomplish all things. This is the pure joy of discipleship.

Follow in Christ's Footsteps

Then he said to his disciples, "The harvest is plentiful, but the laborers are few; therefore pray earnestly to the Lord of the harvest to send out laborers into his harvest."

Matthew 9:37-38 ESV

He replied to him, "Who is my mother, and who are my brothers?" Pointing to his disciples, he said, "Here are my mother and my brothers. For whoever does the will of my Father in heaven is my brother and sister and mother."

Matthew 12:48-50 NIV

At the same time came the disciples unto Jesus, saying, "Who is the greatest in the kingdom of heaven?" And Jesus called a little child unto him, and set him in the midst of them, and said, "Verily I say unto you, except ye be converted, and become as little children, ye shall not enter into the kingdom of heaven. Whosoever therefore shall humble himself as this little child, the same is greatest in the kingdom of heaven."

Matthew 18:1-4 KJV

Then Jesus told his disciples, "If anyone would come after me, let him deny himself and take up his cross and follow me."

Matthew 16:24 ESV

"Go therefore and make disciples of all the nations, baptizing them in the name of the Father and of the Son and of the Holy Spirit."

Matthew 28:19 NKJV

He saith unto them, "Follow me, and I will make you fishers of men."

Matthew 4:19 KJV

So Jesus said to the Jews who had believed in him, "If you abide in my word, you are truly my disciples, and you will know the truth, and the truth will set you free."

John 8:31-32 ESV

"Whoever has my commands and obeys them, he is the one who loves me. He who loves me will be loved by my Father, and I too will love him and show myself to him."

John 14:21 NIV

"If you love me, you will keep my commandments."

John 14:15 ESV

Discipleship

But whoever keeps His word, truly the love of God is perfected in him. By this we know that we are in Him. He who says he abides in Him ought himself also to walk just as He walked.

1 John 2:5-6 NKJV

"Now that I, your Lord and Teacher, have washed your feet, you also should wash one another's feet."

John 13:14 NIV

"Whoever desires to become great among you shall be your servant. And whoever of you desires to be first shall be slave of all. For even the Son of Man did not come to be served, but to serve, and to give His life a ransom for many."

Mark 10:43-45 NKJV

"If any man serve me, let him follow me; and where I am, there shall also my servant be: if any man serve me, him will my Father honour."

John 12:26 KJV

Faith

Now faith is the assurance of things hoped for, the conviction of things not seen.

Hebrews 11:1 ESV

When you struggle with problems, difficulties and disappointments, do you trust God? Are you willing to put your life unconditionally in His hands and confidently trust that whatever He allows in your life will work out for your good?

Jesus Christ came to confirm that God loves you. You are precious in His sight! He wants only what is best for you. When you have this assurance in your heart, you will trust God unconditionally in everything you do.

To ensure peace of mind, place yourself, your plans and your problems in the hands of your Savior. Discuss your problems and secret fears with Him in prayer; talk to Him about the important decisions you have to make. You will then experience the living presence of Christ in every situation. He will lead you and guide you to find rest and peace of mind. Your faith will carry you through in all circumstances.

Have Faith in God

Without faith it is impossible to please God, because anyone who comes to him must believe that he exists and that he rewards those who earnestly seek him.

Hebrews 11:6 NIV

Abram believed the Lord, and he credited it to him as righteousness.

Genesis 15:6 NIV

"Have faith in God," Jesus answered. "I tell you the truth, if anyone says to this mountain, 'Go, throw yourself into the sea,' and does not doubt in his heart but believes that what he says will happen, it will be done for him. Therefore I tell you, whatever you ask for in prayer, believe that you have received it, and it will be yours."

Mark 11:22-24 NIV

We live by faith, not by sight.

2 Corinthians 5:7 NIV

Jesus answered and said to them, "This is the work of God, that you believe in Him whom He sent."

John 6:29 NKJV

Promises from God for Powerful Living

Therefore, since we have been justified by faith, we have peace with God through our Lord Jesus Christ.

Romans 5:1 ESV

If thou shalt confess with thy mouth the Lord Jesus, and shalt believe in thine heart that God hath raised him from the dead, thou shalt be saved. For with the heart man believeth unto righteousness; and with the mouth confession is made unto salvation.

Romans 10:9-10 KJV

So faith comes from hearing, and hearing through the word of Christ.

Romans 10:17 ESV

Trust in the Lord with all thine heart; and lean not unto thine own understanding.

Proverbs 3:5 KJV

By faith we eagerly await through the Spirit the righteousness for which we hope.

Galatians 5:5 NIV

We maintain that a man is justified by faith apart from observing the law.

Romans 3:28 NIV

Faith

The righteous shall live by his faith.

Habakkuk 2:4 ESV

"All things are possible to him who believes."

Mark 9:23 NKJV

For by grace you have been saved through faith, and that not of yourselves; it is the gift of God.

Ephesians 2:8 NKJV

He replied, "Because you have so little faith. I tell you the truth, if you have faith as small as a mustard seed, you can say to this mountain, 'Move from here to there and it will move.' Nothing will be impossible for you."

Matthew 17:20 NIV

These have come so that your faith – of greater worth than gold, which perishes even though refined by fire – may be proved genuine and may result in praise, glory and honor when Jesus Christ is revealed.

1 Peter 1:7 NIV

Finances

Everything in heaven and earth is yours. Yours, O Lord, is the kingdom.

1 Chronicles 29:11 NIV

Wealth can become a blessing or a curse, depending on the priority it has in your life. It is tragic when the acquiring of great wealth becomes the driving force in people's lives.

Whenever money is idolized it destroys everything that is beautiful and worthwhile in terms of character and personality. Being wealthy often causes people to become hard-hearted and contemptuous of those who have nothing.

Money cannot buy those qualities that are essential for abundant life. It might cushion some of life's blows and make life more comfortable, but we must remember that money can buy books, but not intellect; a bed, but not peaceful sleep; food, but not appetite; entertainment, but not happiness; luxuries, but not culture; a Bible, but not heaven. People often forget that the most valuable things in life are free.

What the Word says about Finances

The rich and the poor meet together; the Lord is the Maker of them all.
> Proverbs 22:2 ESV

Better is little with the fear of the Lord than great treasure and trouble therewith. Better is a dinner of herbs where love is, than a stalled ox and hatred therewith.
> Proverbs 15:16-17 KJV

Labour not to be rich: cease from thine own wisdom. Wilt thou set thine eyes upon that which is not? for riches certainly make themselves wings; they fly away as an eagle toward heaven.
> Proverbs 23:4-5 KJV

Whoever loves money never has money enough; whoever loves wealth is never satisfied with his income.
> Ecclesiastes 5:10 NIV

You are enriched in everything for all liberality, which causes thanksgiving through us to God.
> 2 Corinthians 9:11 NKJV

Promises from God for Powerful Living

Remember the Lord your God, for it is he who gives you the ability to produce wealth, and so confirms his covenant, which he swore to your forefathers, as it is today.

Deuteronomy 8:18 NIV

He who does not put out his money at interest and does not take a bribe against the innocent. He who does these things shall never be moved.

Psalm 15:5 ESV

He who is kind to the poor lends to the Lord, and he will reward him for what he has done.

Proverbs 19:17 NIV

Godliness with contentment is great gain. For we brought nothing into this world, and it is certain we can carry nothing out.

1 Timothy 6:6-7 KJV

People who want to get rich fall into temptation and a trap and into many foolish and harmful desires that plunge men into ruin and destruction. For the love of money is a root of all kinds of evil. Some people, eager for money, have wandered from the faith and pierced themselves with many griefs.

1 Timothy 6:9-10 NIV

Finances

Blessed is the one who considers the poor! In the day of trouble the Lord delivers him.

Psalm 41:1 ESV

Command those who are rich in this present age not to be haughty, nor to trust in uncertain riches but in the living God, who gives us richly all things to enjoy.

1 Timothy 6:17 NKJV

Keep your lives free from the love of money and be content with what you have, because God has said, "Never will I leave you; never will I forsake you."

Hebrews 13:5 NIV

Praise the Lord! Blessed is the man who fears the Lord, who greatly delights in his commandments! His offspring will be mighty in the land; the generation of the upright will be blessed. Wealth and riches are in his house, and his righteousness endures forever.

Psalm 112:1-3 ESV

A good man sheweth favour, and lendeth: he will guide his affairs with discretion.

Psalm 112:5 KJV

Forgiveness

"Forgive us our debts, as we also have forgiven our debtors."

Matthew 6:12, ESV

It is one of the great privileges and joys of the Christian faith to know that regardless of what you have done, God is always waiting for you to turn to Him in prayer. His love for you is so vast that you can be assured of His forgiveness even before you enter into His presence. All you have to do is repent and confess your sins to Him.

Many people do not avail themselves of this glorious gift of grace because it seems too simple. Maybe they are too ashamed to confess their failures. However, one thing is sure: the longer you bottle up your guilt, the more difficult it will become to confess your sins.

God knows everything about you, including your weaknesses and despite it all He still loves you. He proved it when Christ died on the cross for you.

Open your heart and lay your guilt before His throne of grace. Here you will experience the balm of His unfathomable love.

Healing Forgiveness

Blessed is he whose transgressions are forgiven, whose sins are covered. Blessed is the man whose sin the Lord does not count against him and in whose spirit is no deceit.

Psalm 32:1-2 NIV

Have mercy upon me, O God, according to Your lovingkindness; according to the multitude of Your tender mercies, blot out my transgressions. Wash me thoroughly from my iniquity, and cleanse me from my sin.

Psalm 51:1-2 NKJV

As far as the east is from the west, so far does he remove our transgressions from us.

Psalm 103:12 ESV

When you were dead in your sins and in the uncircumcision of your sinful nature, God made you alive with Christ. He forgave us all our sins, having canceled the written code, with its regulations, that was against us and that stood opposed to us; he took it away, nailing it to the cross.

Colossians 2:13-14 NIV

Promises from God for Powerful Living

Who is a God like unto thee, that pardoneth iniquity, and passeth by the transgression of the remnant of his heritage? he retaineth not his anger for ever, because he delighteth in mercy. He will turn again, he will have compassion upon us; he will subdue our iniquities; and thou wilt cast all their sins into the depths of the sea.

Micah 7:18-19 KJV

"If your brother sins, rebuke him, and if he repents, forgive him. If he sins against you seven times in a day, and seven times comes back to you and says, 'I repent,' forgive him."

Luke 17:3-4 NIV

"For I will be merciful toward their iniquities, and I will remember their sins no more."

Hebrews 8:12 ESV

In him we have redemption through his blood, the forgiveness of sins, in accordance with the riches of God's grace.

Ephesians 1:7 NIV

Be kind to one another, tenderhearted, forgiving one another, even as God in Christ forgave you.

Ephesians 4:32 NKJV

Forgiveness

If we confess our sins, he is faithful and just to forgive us our sins, and to cleanse us from all unrighteousness.

1 John 1:9 KJV

"Come now, let us reason together, says the Lord: though your sins are like scarlet, they shall be as white as snow; though they are red like crimson, they shall become like wool."

Isaiah 1:18 ESV

Bear with each other and forgive whatever grievances you may have against one another. Forgive as the Lord forgave you.

Colossians 3:13 NIV

Then Peter came to Jesus and asked, "Lord, how many times shall I forgive my brother when he sins against me? Up to seven times?" Jesus answered, "I tell you, not seven times, but seventy-seven times."

Matthew 18:21-22 NIV

"Whenever you stand praying, forgive, if you have anything against anyone, so that your Father also who is in heaven may forgive you your trespasses."

Mark 11:25 ESV

Freedom

Out of my distress I called on the Lord; the Lord answered me and set me free.

Psalm 118:5 ESV

Have you ever felt that you are not reaching your potential? You might be frustrated because of the monotonous routine of your life. Nothing exciting ever happens and life has lost its beauty and sparkle. Your life is probably being shrouded by increasing trivialities that are suffocating all rightful ambition within you.

Do not carry on through life bound by a mediocre existence while the Holy Spirit can offer you so much more.

When the Holy Spirit comes into your life and takes control, you can expect radical changes. Through the Holy Spirit you will become more aware of the needs of others and start living a life of unselfish service. Your life will have meaning and purpose and you will be empowered by an indescribable feeling of real freedom. Your traveling companion, the Holy Spirit, is not only your guide, but also the One who protects and inspires you!

Freedom in Christ

Then Jesus said to those Jews who believed Him, "If you abide in My word, you are My disciples indeed. And you shall know the truth, and the truth shall make you free."

John 8:31-32 NKJV

"Heal the sick, raise the dead, cleanse those who have leprosy, drive out demons. Freely you have received, freely give."

Matthew 10:8 NIV

The Spirit of the Sovereign Lord is on me, because the Lord has anointed me to preach good news to the poor. He has sent me to bind up the brokenhearted, to proclaim freedom for the captives and release from darkness for the prisoners.

Isaiah 61:1 NIV

For the creation was subjected to frustration, not by its own choice, but by the will of the one who subjected it, in hope that the creation itself will be liberated from its bondage to decay and brought into the glorious freedom of the children of God.

Romans 8:20-21 NIV

Promises from God for Powerful Living

And I will walk at liberty: for I seek thy precepts.

Psalm 119:45 KJV

Now the Lord is the Spirit; and where the Spirit of the Lord is, there is liberty.

2 Corinthians 3:17 NKJV

For freedom Christ has set us free; stand firm therefore, and do not submit again to a yoke of slavery.

Galatians 5:1 ESV

"Come to me, all you who are weary and burdened, and I will give you rest. Take my yoke upon you and learn from me, for I am gentle and humble in heart, and you will find rest for your souls. For my yoke is easy and my burden is light."

Matthew 11:28-30 NIV

For you, brethren, have been called to liberty; only do not use liberty as an opportunity for the flesh, but through love serve one another.

Galatians 5:13 NKJV

"I am pure, without transgression; I am clean, and there is no iniquity in me."

Job 33:9 ESV

Freedom

But whoso looketh into the perfect law of liberty, and continueth therein, he being not a forgetful hearer, but a doer of the work, this man shall be blessed in his deed.

James 1:25 KJV

Through Christ Jesus the law of the Spirit of life set me free from the law of sin and death.

Romans 8:2 NIV

I run in the path of your commands, for you have set my heart free.

Psalm 119:32 NIV

The Lord is righteous; He has cut in pieces the cords of the wicked.

Psalm 129:4 NKJV

In him and through faith in him we may approach God with freedom and confidence.

Ephesians 3:12 NIV

Now that you have been set free from sin and have become slaves of God, the fruit you get leads to sanctification and its end, eternal life.

Romans 6:22 ESV

God's Care

*Praise be to the L*ORD*, to God our Savior, who daily bears our burdens.*

Psalm 68:19 NIV

Our eyes are extremely sensitive and must be protected. In Psalm 17:6-8 David asks the Lord to protect him as the apple of His eye.

He asks God to protect him because he believes that God will answer his prayers. He sees God, compassionate and interested, bending down to listen to his prayer. He believes that God will use His power to protect him. As David looks to God with eyes of expectation, he receives the protection he so desperately sought.

Use David's prayer to remind yourself that God lovingly and faithfully protects you. He is the only One who can truly shield and protect you. In prayer, lay your troubles at His feet because He cares for you.

God's Compassionate Care

Know therefore that the Lord thy God, he is God, the faithful God, which keepeth covenant and mercy with them that love him and keep his commandments to a thousand generations.

Deuteronomy 7:9 KJV

Cast all your anxiety on him because he cares for you.

1 Peter 5:7 NIV

We know that in all things God works for the good of those who love him, who have been called according to his purpose.

Romans 8:28 NIV

What is man that you are mindful of him, the son of man that you care for him? You made him a little lower than the heavenly beings and crowned him with glory and honor.

Psalm 8:4-5 NIV

For he is our God, and we are the people of his pasture, and the sheep of his hand.

Psalm 95:7 ESV

Promises from God for Powerful Living

Cast thy burden upon the L<small>ORD</small>, and he shall sustain thee: he shall never suffer the righteous to be moved.

Psalm 55:22 KJV

You visit the earth and water it; you greatly enrich it; the river of God is full of water; you provide their grain, for so you have prepared it.

Psalm 65:9 ESV

This is what the Sovereign L<small>ORD</small> says: "I myself will search for my sheep and look after them. As a shepherd looks after his scattered flock when he is with them, so will I look after my sheep. I will rescue them from all the places where they were scattered on a day of clouds and darkness."

Ezekiel 34:11-12 NIV

The L<small>ORD</small> is good, a strong hold in the day of trouble; and he knoweth them that trust in him.

Nahum 1:7 KJV

He will feed His flock like a shepherd; He will gather the lambs with His arm, and carry them in His bosom, and gently lead those who are with young.

Isaiah 40:11 NKJV

God's Care

The LORD is my shepherd, I shall not be in want. He makes me lie down in green pastures, he leads me beside quiet waters, he restores my soul. He guides me in paths of righteousness for his name's sake. Even though I walk through the valley of the shadow of death, I will fear no evil, for you are with me; your rod and your staff, they comfort me.

Psalm 23:1-4 NIV

Blessed be the God and Father of our Lord Jesus Christ, the Father of mercies and God of all comfort.

2 Corinthians 1:3 ESV

The LORD your God, who is going before you, will fight for you, as he did for you in Egypt, before your very eyes, and in the desert. There you saw how the LORD your God carried you, as a father carries his son, all the way you went until you reached this place.

Deuteronomy 1:30-31 NIV

"Can a mother forget the baby at her breast and have no compassion on the child she has borne? Though she may forget, I will not forget you!"

Isaiah 49:15 NIV

God's Will

Teach me to do thy will; for thou art my God: thy spirit is good; lead me into the land of uprightness.
Psalm 143:10 KJV

To surrender our lives to the will of God can be a formidable challenge. At times, our personal dreams and aspirations are in conflict with God's will for us.

Jesus wrestled in prayer about this issue in the Garden of Gethsemane. God's method to ensure the redemption of humankind was at stake and involved suffering and crucifixion. Jesus saw the difficult road ahead and spent a night of torment in prayer about it. The courage and strength He found in prayer that night helped Him to face the suffering He had to endure the next day.

The choices we make are of far less importance than the choices Jesus had to make. As His will becomes clear to us, may God help us to surrender to His perfect will, following the example of our Lord and Master, Jesus Christ.

Teach Us to do Thy Will

Do not conform any longer to the pattern of this world, but be transformed by the renewing of your mind. Then you will be able to test and approve what God's will is – his good, pleasing and perfect will.

Romans 12:2 NIV

I delight to do thy will, O my God: yea, thy law is within my heart.

Psalm 40:8 KJV

"My food is to do the will of Him who sent Me, and to finish His work."

John 4:34 NKJV

He made known to us the mystery of his will according to his good pleasure, which he purposed in Christ, to be put into effect when the times will have reached their fulfillment – to bring all things in heaven and on earth together under one head, even Christ.

Ephesians 1:9-10 NIV

For this is the will of God, your sanctification.

1 Thessalonians 4:3 ESV

Be joyful always; pray continually; give thanks in all circumstances, for this is God's will for you in Christ Jesus.

1 Thessalonians 5:16-18 NIV

The world and its desires pass away, but the man who does the will of God lives forever.

1 John 2:17 NIV

"Your kingdom come, your will be done, on earth as it is in heaven."

Matthew 6:10 ESV

Going a little farther, he fell with his face to the ground and prayed, "My Father, if it is possible, may this cup be taken from me. Yet not as I will, but as you will."

Matthew 26:39 NIV

There are many devices in a man's heart; nevertheless the counsel of the Lord, that shall stand.

Proverbs 19:21 KJV

O Lord, You are my God. I will exalt You, I will praise Your name, for You have done wonderful things; your counsels of old are faithfulness and truth.

Isaiah 25:1 NKJV

God's Will

"I am God, and there is no other; I am God, and there is none like me. I make known the end from the beginning, from ancient times, what is still to come. I say: My purpose will stand, and I will do all that I please. From the east I summon a bird of prey; from a far-off land, a man to fulfill my purpose. What I have said, that will I bring about; what I have planned, that will I do."

Isaiah 46:9-11 NIV

For it is God which worketh in you both to will and to do of his good pleasure.

Philippians 2:13 KJV

Whatever the LORD pleases He does, in heaven and in earth, in the seas and in all deep places.

Psalm 135:6 NKJV

Obey them not only to win their favor when their eye is on you, but like slaves of Christ, doing the will of God from your heart.

Ephesians 6:6 NIV

You need to persevere so that when you have done the will of God, you will receive what he has promised.

Hebrews 10:36 NIV

Goodness

Do good, O Lord, to those who are good, to those who are upright in heart.

Psalm 125:4 NIV

Good works are the by-product of a Christian lifestyle. It is impossible to live with the awareness of the presence of Christ and still do evil deeds. Jesus Christ becomes the mold according to which you cast your life.

Many dedicated Christians believe that performing noble deeds will eventually get them into heaven. We must remember, however, that many agnostics and atheists are "good" people who help the poor and who find joy in doing this.

These people are good because being a good person has been cultivated in them. Christians, on the other hand, live in a vital relationship with the living Christ and are good because the life of their Master is reflected in and through them. The difference between human goodness and a life inspired by Christ is the spiritual dimension found in the lives of Christians. A life inspired by the Holy Spirit rises above natural goodness and makes Jesus Christ visible in our lives.

Experiencing God's Goodness

The trumpeters and singers joined in unison, as with one voice, to give praise and thanks to the Lord. Accompanied by trumpets, cymbals and other instruments, they raised their voices in praise to the Lord and sang: "He is good; his love endures forever." Then the temple of the Lord was filled with a cloud.

2 Chronicles 5:13 NIV

"A good man out of the good treasure of his heart brings forth good; and an evil man out of the evil treasure of his heart brings forth evil. For out of the abundance of the heart his mouth speaks."

Luke 6:45 NKJV

I myself am satisfied about you, my brothers, that you yourselves are full of goodness, filled with all knowledge and able to instruct one another.

Romans 15:14 ESV

The Lord is good to all, and his mercy is over all that he has made.

Psalm 145:9 ESV

Promises from God for Powerful Living

His divine power has given to us all things that pertain to life and godliness, through the knowledge of Him who called us by glory and virtue.

2 Peter 1:3 NKJV

God is able to make all grace abound toward you; that ye, always having all sufficiency in all things, may abound to every good work.

2 Corinthians 9:8 KJV

May our Lord Jesus Christ himself and God our Father, who loved us and by his grace gave us eternal encouragement and good hope, encourage your hearts and strengthen you in every good deed and word.

2 Thessalonians 2:16-17 NIV

We pray this in order that you may live a life worthy of the Lord and may please him in every way: bearing fruit in every good work, growing in the knowledge of God.

Colossians 1:10 NIV

"When you give to the needy, do not let your left hand know what your right hand is doing, so that your giving may be in secret. Then your Father, who sees what is done in secret, will reward you."

Matthew 6:3-4 NIV

Goodness

Let ours also learn to maintain good works for necessary uses, that they be not unfruitful.

Titus 3:14 KJV

Surely goodness and mercy shall follow me all the days of my life: and I will dwell in the house of the Lord for ever.

Psalm 23:6 KJV

We know that in all things God works for the good of those who love him, who have been called according to his purpose.

Romans 8:28 NIV

At one time you were darkness, but now you are light in the Lord. Walk as children of light (for the fruit of light is found in all that is good and right and true).

Ephesians 5:8-9 ESV

Let your light so shine before men, that they may see your good works and glorify your Father in heaven.

Matthew 5:16 NKJV

For we are God's workmanship, created in Christ Jesus to do good works, which God prepared in advance for us to do.

Ephesians 2:10 NIV

GRACE

The grace of our Lord was poured out on me abundantly, along with the faith and love that are in Christ Jesus.
1 Timothy 1:14 NIV

Amazing Grace is surely one of the best-loved hymns of all times. It tells about a prodigal son who came back into the Father's house. John Newton, the hymn writer, wrote that he was spiritually blind and lost, but the grace of God touched and healed him. This hymn tells of a redeeming God whose love is so great that He gave His all through grace.

As you meditate on Christ's sacrifice, you come face to face with the greatest act of compassion and love that this world has ever known: the Son of God took our guilt upon Himself and sacrificed His life so that we could be redeemed from sin.

But His grace extends further than that. Even though people are forgetful and often drift away from God, Christ waits patiently and lovingly for us to turn back to Him.

You can express your gratitude for His boundless love by showing others the same grace and mercy that Jesus has shown to you.

God's Abundant Grace

The Word was made flesh, and dwelt among us, (and we beheld his glory, the glory as of the only begotten of the Father,) full of grace and truth.

John 1:14 KJV

And of his fulness have all we received, and grace for grace. For the law was given by Moses, but grace and truth came by Jesus Christ.

John 1:16-17 KJV

God, being rich in mercy, because of the great love with which he loved us, even when we were dead in our trespasses, made us alive together with Christ – by grace you have been saved.

Ephesians 2:4-5 ESV

By the grace of God I am what I am, and His grace toward me was not in vain; but I labored more abundantly than they all, yet not I, but the grace of God which was with me.

1 Corinthians 15:10 NKJV

For by grace you have been saved through faith, and that not of yourselves; it is the gift of God, not of works, lest anyone should boast.

Ephesians 2:8-9 NKJV

Grow in the grace and knowledge of our Lord and Savior Jesus Christ. To him be glory both now and to the day of eternity. Amen.

2 Peter 3:18 ESV

You therefore, my son, be strong in the grace that is in Christ Jesus.

2 Timothy 2:1 NKJV

So do not be ashamed to testify about our Lord, or ashamed of me his prisoner. But join with me in suffering for the gospel, by the power of God, who has saved us and called us to a holy life – not because of anything we have done but because of his own purpose and grace. This grace was given us in Christ Jesus before the beginning of time.

2 Timothy 1:8-9 NIV

I thank my God always on your behalf, for the grace of God which is given you by Jesus Christ.

1 Corinthians 1:4 KJV

Grace

For you know the grace of our Lord Jesus Christ, that though he was rich, yet for your sakes he became poor, so that you through his poverty might become rich.

2 Corinthians 8:9 NIV

He said to me, "My grace is sufficient for you, for my power is made perfect in weakness." Therefore I will boast all the more gladly about my weaknesses, so that Christ's power may rest upon me.

2 Corinthians 12:9 NIV

The grace of the Lord Jesus Christ, and the love of God, and the communion of the Holy Ghost, be with you all. Amen.

2 Corinthians 13:14 KJV

Therefore, since we have been justified through faith, we have peace with God through our Lord Jesus Christ, through whom we have gained access by faith into this grace in which we now stand. And we rejoice in the hope of the glory of God.

Romans 5:1-2 NIV

Let us therefore come boldly unto the throne of grace, that we may obtain mercy, and find grace to help in time of need.

Hebrews 4:16 KJV

Guidance

Shew me thy ways, O Lord; teach me thy paths.
Psalm 25:4 KJV

Many people think that God's guidance is covered by a cloud of mysticism. When they encounter problems they pray fervently for God to guide them, but when things are back to normal, they confidently make their own decisions.

By doing this they're ignoring the value God's guidance has for routine matters of life. They are not cultivating a close relationship with the Father, because this is only developed through ongoing obedience to His all-wise guidance.

God often guides us through our common sense, but we often do not recognize it as His guidance. It needs to be inspired through an active prayer life. This brings your mind and thoughts into harmony with God. Then, bit by bit, your whole life comes under God's control.

If you seek His guidance in the small issues of life, it will be much easier to recognize His will when important decisions have to be made.

May God Guide You

He maketh me to lie down in green pastures: he leadeth me beside the still waters. He restoreth my soul: he leadeth me in the paths of righteousness for his name's sake.

Psalm 23:2-3 KJV

Trust in the Lord and do good; dwell in the land and enjoy safe pasture. Delight yourself in the Lord and he will give you the desires of your heart. Commit your way to the Lord; trust in him and he will do this.

Psalm 37:3-5 NIV

The steps of a man are established by the Lord, when he delights in his way; though he fall, he shall not be cast headlong, for the Lord upholds his hand.

Psalm 37:23-24 ESV

Let the morning bring me word of your unfailing love, for I have put my trust in you. Show me the way I should go, for to you I lift up my soul. Teach me to do your will, for you are my God; may your good Spirit lead me on level ground.

Psalm 143:8, 10 NIV

You have made known to me the path of life;
you will fill me with joy in your presence,
with eternal pleasures at your right hand.

Psalm 16:11 NIV

I will run the course of Your commandments, for You shall enlarge my heart.

Psalm 119:32 NKJV

Your word is a lamp to my feet and a light for my path.

Psalm 119:105 NIV

That thou mayest walk in the way of good men, and keep the paths of the righteous.

Proverbs 2:20 KJV

The path of the just is like the shining sun, that shines ever brighter unto the perfect day.

Proverbs 4:18 NKJV

You have made known to me the paths of life; you will fill me with joy in your presence.

Acts 2:28 NIV

"Stand at the crossroads and look; ask for the ancient paths, ask where the good way is, and walk in it."

Jeremiah 6:16 NIV

Guidance

"But when he, the Spirit of truth, comes, he will guide you into all truth. He will not speak on his own; he will speak only what he hears, and he will tell you what is yet to come."

John 16:13 NIV

"I will instruct thee and teach thee in the way which thou shalt go: I will guide thee with mine eye."

Psalm 32:8 KJV

For this is God, our God forever and ever; He will be our guide even to death.

Psalm 48:14 NKJV

The heart of man plans his way, but the Lord establishes his steps.

Proverbs 16:9 ESV

Trust in the Lord with all your heart, and lean not on your own understanding; in all your ways acknowledge Him, and He shall direct your paths.

Proverbs 3:5-6 NKJV

The precepts of the Lord are right, giving joy to the heart. The commands of the Lord are radiant, giving light to the eyes.

Psalm 19:8 NIV

Heaven

"Blessed are the poor in spirit, for theirs is the kingdom of heaven."

Matthew 5:3 ESV

It is amazing how some people only live from day to day without any thought of tomorrow. Others might plan their financial matters carefully, yet refuse to think about the certainty of death.

It is astounding how many people pay serious attention to the development of their earthly plans, but seldom think about leaving this world and entering eternity.

To say that it is impossible to plan for eternity because we know nothing about it is not a logical response. The Scriptures clearly teach us the truth about the spiritual world. Jesus spoke of heaven in clear and lucid terms and His words should be enough for anyone thinking seriously about this matter.

To look at life from the perspective of eternity is to give new meaning to your daily life. You will then be inclined to fulfill your daily duty to the honor of God and live your whole life so that it is pleasing to Him.

Your Heavenly Home

"In my Father's house are many rooms; if it were not so, I would have told you. I am going there to prepare a place for you. And if I go and prepare a place for you, I will come back and take you to be with me that you also may be where I am."

John 14:2-3 NIV

You have come to Mount Zion, to the heavenly Jerusalem, the city of the living God. You have come to thousands upon thousands of angels in joyful assembly, to the church of the firstborn, whose names are written in heaven. You have come to God, the judge of all men, to the spirits of righteous men made perfect.

Hebrews 12:22-23 NIV

For here we have no lasting city, but we seek the city that is to come.

Hebrews 13:14 ESV

"Heaven is my throne, and the earth is my footstool. What kind of house will you build for me? says the Lord. Or where will my resting place be?"

Acts 7:49 NIV

Promises from God for Powerful Living

Blessed be the God and Father of our Lord Jesus Christ, which according to his abundant mercy hath begotten us again unto a lively hope by the resurrection of Jesus Christ from the dead, to an inheritance incorruptible, and undefiled, and that fadeth not away, reserved in heaven for you.

1 Peter 1:3-4 KJV

"He who has an ear, let him hear what the Spirit says to the churches. To him who overcomes, I will give the right to eat from the tree of life, which is in the paradise of God."

Revelation 2:7 NIV

Our citizenship is in heaven. And we eagerly await a Savior from there, the Lord Jesus Christ, who, by the power that enables him to bring everything under his control, will transform our lowly bodies so that they will be like his glorious body.

Philippians 3:20-21 NIV

Therefore know this day, and consider it in your heart, that the Lord Himself is God in heaven above and on the earth beneath; there is no other.

Deuteronomy 4:39 NKJV

Heaven

If then you were raised with Christ, seek those things which are above, where Christ is, sitting at the right hand of God. Set your mind on things above, not on things on the earth.

Colossians 3:1-2 NKJV

The throne of God and of the Lamb will be in the city, and his servants will serve him. They will see his face, and his name will be on their foreheads. There will be no more night. They will not need the light of a lamp or the light of the sun, for the Lord God will give them light. And they will reign for ever and ever.

Revelation 22:3-5 NIV

Dominion and awe belong to God; he establishes order in the heights of heaven.

Job 25:2 NIV

The Lord looks down from heaven upon the children of men, to see if there are any who understand, who seek God.

Psalm 14:2 NKJV

As you go, preach this message: "The kingdom of heaven is near."

Matthew 10:7 NIV

HOLINESS

Follow peace with all men, and holiness, without which no man shall see the Lord.

Hebrews 12:14 KJV

Many people believe that living a holy life will cause them to miss out on the fun in life. They find it hard to believe that a life of fullness, joy and abundance is the result of holiness. Yet, true holiness is the most dynamic, creative and meaningful force in the world.

To be holy means to live in the right relationship with God. Developing a deep understanding of God causes you to enjoy life to the full and also gives you a greater understanding of people.

Holiness encourages you to live in the power of the Holy Spirit and results in a balanced approach to life. Nobody who strives to be holy will ever find life boring, because they are living for the King.

The secret of a balanced and enjoyable life is to live so that it is easy for the Master to reveal Himself through you. This is the way of true sanctification and the road to a successful life.

Striving for Holiness

"For I am the Lord your God: ye shall therefore sanctify yourselves, and ye shall be holy; for I am holy: neither shall ye defile yourselves with any manner of creeping thing that creepeth upon the earth."

Leviticus 11:44 KJV

So do not be ashamed to testify about our Lord, or ashamed of me his prisoner. But join with me in suffering for the gospel, by the power of God, who has saved us and called us to a holy life – not because of anything we have done but because of his own purpose and grace. This grace was given us in Christ Jesus before the beginning of time.

2 Timothy 1:8-9 NIV

They were calling to one another: "Holy, holy, holy is the Lord Almighty; the whole earth is full of his glory."

Isaiah 6:3 NIV

Such a high priest meets our need – one who is holy, blameless, pure, set apart from sinners, exalted above the heavens.

Hebrews 7:26 NIV

Now having been set free from sin, and having become slaves of God, you have your fruit to holiness, and the end, everlasting life.

Romans 6:22 NKJV

Since we have these promises, beloved, let us cleanse ourselves from every defilement of body and spirit, bringing holiness to completion in the fear of God.

2 Corinthians 7:1 ESV

God has not called us for impurity, but in holiness. Therefore whoever disregards this, disregards not man but God, who gives his Holy Spirit to you.

1 Thessalonians 4:7-8 ESV

You are a chosen generation, a royal priesthood, a holy nation, His own special people, that you may proclaim the praises of Him who called you out of darkness into His marvelous light.

1 Peter 2:9 NKJV

For you are a people holy to the Lord your God. The Lord your God has chosen you out of all the peoples on the face of the earth to be his people, his treasured possession.

Deuteronomy 7:6 NIV

Holiness

"Therefore come out from them and be separate," says the Lord. "Touch no unclean thing, and I will receive you. I will be a Father to you, and you will be my sons and daughters, says the Lord Almighty."

2 Corinthians 6:17-18 NIV

Do everything without complaining or arguing, so that you may become blameless and pure, children of God without fault in a crooked and depraved generation, in which you shine like the stars in the universe.

Philippians 2:14-15 NIV

Who is like unto thee, O Lord, among the gods? who is like thee, glorious in holiness, fearful in praises, doing wonders?

Exodus 15:11 KJV

For thus saith the high and lofty One that inhabiteth eternity, whose name is Holy; "I dwell in the high and holy place, with him also that is of a contrite and humble spirit, to revive the spirit of the humble, and to revive the heart of the contrite ones."

Isaiah 57:15 KJV

Inheritance

"Blessed are the meek, for they will inherit the earth."
Matthew 5:5 NIV

Do you sometimes feel uncertain of your faith? You might feel tempted to give up trying to be a disciple or fellowshiping with Christ's followers.

You should, however, never forget that there are two distinct sides to your Christian life: God's side and yours. It was God who called you to live in harmony with Him. You responded to His call and became a Christian. This alone is reason enough for you to stand strong in your faith.

You belong to the living Savior: He bought you with His blood and accepted you as His own. Always remember your rich inheritance and the kind of life God has called you to. This world might offer you attractive temptations but remember who and what you are in Christ.

You have been chosen; you belong to a royal priesthood and you have been set apart. Muster all the strength you possess to be true to this noble calling and remember that God will never let go of you!

Priceless Inheritance

And you also were included in Christ when you heard the word of truth, the gospel of your salvation. Having believed, you were marked in him with a seal, the promised Holy Spirit, who is a deposit guaranteeing our inheritance until the redemption of those who are God's possession – to the praise of his glory.

Ephesians 1:13-14 NIV

The lines are fallen unto me in pleasant places; yea, I have a goodly heritage.

Psalm 16:6 KJV

Wait for the LORD and keep his way. He will exalt you to inherit the land; when the wicked are cut off, you will see it.

Psalm 37:34 NIV

Remember me, O LORD, when you show favor to your people, come to my aid when you save them, that I may enjoy the prosperity of your chosen ones, that I may share in the joy of your nation and join your inheritance in giving praise.

Psalm 106:4-5 NIV

Promises from God for Powerful Living

But as it is written, Eye hath not seen, nor ear heard, neither have entered into the heart of man, the things which God hath prepared for them that love him.

1 Corinthians 2:9 KJV

Listen, my dear brothers: Has not God chosen those who are poor in the eyes of the world to be rich in faith and to inherit the kingdom he promised those who love him?

James 2:5 NIV

If you are Christ's, then you are Abraham's offspring, heirs according to promise.

Galatians 3:29 ESV

That ye be not slothful, but followers of them who through faith and patience inherit the promises.

Hebrews 6:12 KJV

Blessed be the God and Father of our Lord Jesus Christ, who according to His abundant mercy has begotten us again to a living hope through the resurrection of Jesus Christ from the dead, to an inheritance incorruptible and undefiled and that does not fade away, reserved in heaven for you.

1 Peter 1:3-4 NKJV

Inheritance

For the Lord will not forsake his people; he will not abandon his heritage.

Psalm 94:14 ESV

He is the Mediator of the new covenant, by means of death, for the redemption of the transgressions under the first covenant, that those who are called may receive the promise of the eternal inheritance.

Hebrews 9:15 NKJV

But the Scripture imprisoned everything under sin, so that the promise by faith in Jesus Christ might be given to those who believe.

Galatians 3:22 ESV

I pray also that the eyes of your heart may be enlightened in order that you may know the hope to which he has called you, the riches of his glorious inheritance in the saints.

Ephesians 1:18 NIV

Because you are sons, God sent the Spirit of his Son into our hearts, the Spirit who calls out, "Abba, Father." So you are no longer a slave, but a son; and since you are a son, God has made you also an heir.

Galatians 4:6-7 NIV

Jesus Christ

"I am the resurrection and the life. Whoever believes in me, though he die, yet shall he live, and everyone who lives and believes in me shall never die."

John 11:25-26 ESV

It is fundamental to the Christian faith that Jesus Christ, the Son of God, became a human being and was born as a baby, lived on earth, died and was buried. He was then resurrected from the dead and ascended to heaven. If this had not happened the Lord would have remained inaccessible to ordinary people.

God, in His infinite wisdom and love for the world, took on human form and came to live among people. If God had not become human we would never have known the dynamic impact of Jesus Christ on humankind. We would still be walking in darkness.

As a disciple of Jesus your life should reflect Him. The Holy Spirit enables you to follow Him and your task is made easier by the knowledge that Jesus understands because He has walked the same road that you are walking now.

Jesus Christ, Our Redeemer

In the beginning was the Word, and the Word was with God, and the Word was God. In him was life; and the life was the light of men.

John 1:1, 4 KJV

He was pierced for our transgressions, he was crushed for our iniquities; the punishment that brought us peace was upon him, and by his wounds we are healed.

Isaiah 53:5 NIV

For there is one God and one mediator between God and men, the man Christ Jesus, who gave himself as a ransom for all men.

1 Timothy 2:5-6 NIV

For by Him all things were created that are in heaven and that are on earth, visible and invisible, whether thrones or dominions or principalities or powers. All things were created through Him and for Him. And He is before all things, and in Him all things consist.

Colossians 1:16-17 NKJV

Promises from God for Powerful Living

He is the image of the invisible God, the firstborn of all creation. For in him all the fullness of God was pleased to dwell.

Colossians 1:15, 19 ESV

For unto us a child is born, unto us a son is given: and the government shall be upon his shoulder: and his name shall be called The mighty God, The Prince of Peace.

Isaiah 9:6 KJV

Such a High Priest was fitting for us, who is holy, harmless, undefiled, separate from sinners, and has become higher than the heavens.

Hebrews 7:26 NKJV

"I am the good shepherd. The good shepherd lays down his life for the sheep."

John 10:11 ESV

"For God so loved the world that he gave his one and only Son, that whoever believes in him shall not perish but have eternal life."

John 3:16 NIV

God was pleased through him to reconcile to himself all things, by making peace through his blood, shed on the cross.

Colossians 1:19-20 NIV

Jesus Christ

God demonstrates His own love toward us, in that while we were still sinners, Christ died for us.

Romans 5:8 NKJV

When the centurion and those with him who were guarding Jesus saw the earthquake and all that had happened, they were terrified, and exclaimed, "Surely he was the Son of God!"

Matthew 27:54 NIV

We preach Christ crucified. But to those whom God has called, Christ the power of God and the wisdom of God.

1 Corinthians 1:23-24 NIV

Yet to all who received him, to those who believed in his name, he gave the right to become children of God.

John 1:12 NIV

Jesus said, "I am the way, and the truth, and the life. No one comes to the Father except through me."

John 14:6 ESV

Simon Peter answered and said, "Thou art the Christ, the Son of the living God."

Matthew 16:16 KJV

The Kingdom of God

Since we are receiving a kingdom that cannot be shaken, let us be thankful, and so worship God acceptably with reverence and awe!

Hebrews 12:28 NIV

The kingdom of God is found in the hearts of those in whom Jesus Christ reigns as King. It is the kingdom of good relationships, because you are reconciled with God and living in harmony with Him through the power and love of Jesus. This then enables you to live in peace with your fellowmen.

Only when the risen Lord reigns supreme in the lives of people can His kingdom be established in their thoughts, spirits and emotions. God requires unconditional obedience and assurance of your faithfulness. This faithfulness shouldn't be an emotional one-time vow, but a daily commitment to Him, regardless of your emotional state.

When the King makes His power known, you experience His strength, joy, peace and all His other gifts in your daily life. The greatest joy in life is the assurance that you belong to Him and He to you, because He lives in you through His Holy Spirit.

What the Word Says About the Kingdom of God

"But seek ye first the kingdom of God, and his righteousness; and all these things shall be added unto you."

Matthew 6:33 KJV

Your throne, O God, is forever and ever; A scepter of righteousness is the scepter of Your kingdom.

Psalm 45:6 NKJV

O Lord God of our fathers, art not thou God in heaven? and rulest not thou over all the kingdoms of the heathen? and in thine hand is there not power and might, so that none is able to withstand thee?

2 Chronicles 20:6 KJV

"O Lord Almighty, God of Israel, enthroned between the cherubim, you alone are God over all the kingdoms of the earth. You have made heaven and earth."

Isaiah 37:16 NIV

"Blessed are the poor in spirit: for theirs is the kingdom of heaven."

Matthew 5:3 KJV

Promises from God for Powerful Living

After this, Jesus traveled about from one town and village to another, proclaiming the good news of the kingdom of God. The Twelve were with him.

Luke 8:1 NIV

He sent them out to preach the kingdom of God and to heal the sick.

Luke 9:2 NIV

Again he asked, "What shall I compare the kingdom of God to? It is like yeast that a woman took and mixed into a large amount of flour until it worked all through the dough."

Luke 13:20-21 NIV

"People will come from east and west and north and south, and will take their places at the feast in the kingdom of God."

Luke 13:29 NIV

"Blessed is everyone who will eat bread in the kingdom of God!"

Luke 14:15 ESV

For the kingdom of God is not a matter of eating and drinking, but of righteousness, peace and joy in the Holy Spirit.

Romans 14:17 NIV

The Kingdom of God

"The time has come," he said. "The kingdom of God is near. Repent and believe the good news!"

Mark 1:15 NIV

Again he said, "What shall we say the kingdom of God is like, or what parable shall we use to describe it? It is like a mustard seed, which is the smallest seed you plant in the ground. Yet when planted, it grows and becomes the largest of all garden plants, with such big branches that the birds of the air can perch in its shade."

Mark 4:30-32 NIV

When Jesus saw it, he was indignant and said to them, "Do not hinder them, for to such belongs the kingdom of God. Truly, I say to you, whoever does not receive the kingdom of God like a child shall not enter it."

Mark 10:14-15 ESV

When he was demanded of the Pharisees, when the kingdom of God should come, he answered them and said, "The kingdom of God cometh not with observation: Neither shall they say, Lo here! or, lo there! for, behold, the kingdom of God is within you."

Luke 17:20-21 KJV

LIFE

I have been crucified with Christ and I no longer live, but Christ lives in me. The life I live in the body, I live by faith in the Son of God, who loved me and gave himself for me.

Galatians 2:20 NIV

God granted you a privilege beyond words. He called upon you to share in the life of His Son, Jesus, the living Christ. Once the full meaning of this divine grace has dawned upon you, the implications are almost too vast to assimilate with our human minds.

To share in the life of Christ opens up immense possibilities for us, but also huge responsibilities. Linked to such an infinite force and holy wisdom, is the glorious fact that your understanding of God deepens, your vision of what your life could be broadens and you become aware of the constant presence of Christ in your life.

The holy characteristics of God must be revealed through your life in love, honesty, selflessness and integrity. Christ sacrificed Himself so that you can share your life with Him.

A Spirit-filled Life

"The thief comes only to steal and kill and destroy; I have come that they may have life, and have it to the full."

John 10:10 NIV

The Lord God formed man of the dust of the ground, and breathed into his nostrils the breath of life; and man became a living soul.

Genesis 2:7 KJV

He answered and said, "It is written, 'Man shall not live by bread alone, but by every word that proceeds from the mouth of God.'"

Matthew 4:4 NKJV

I call heaven and earth to record this day against you, that I have set before you life and death, blessing and cursing: therefore choose life, that both thou and thy seed may live.

Deuteronomy 30:19 KJV

"For I know that my Redeemer lives, and at the last he will stand upon the earth."

Job 19:25 ESV

"For the gate is narrow and the way is hard that leads to life, and those who find it are few."

Matthew 7:14 ESV

"For what is a man profited, if he shall gain the whole world, and lose his own soul? or what shall a man give in exchange for his soul?"

Matthew 16:26 KJV

"I tell you the truth, whoever hears my word and believes him who sent me has eternal life and will not be condemned; he has crossed over from death to life."

John 5:24 NIV

Simon Peter answered him, "Lord, to whom shall we go? You have the words of eternal life."

John 6:68 NIV

"I give unto them eternal life; and they shall never perish, neither shall any man pluck them out of my hand."

John 10:28 KJV

He who has the Son has life; he who does not have the Son of God does not have life.

1 John 5:12 NIV

Life

Because your love is better than life, my lips will glorify you.

Psalm 63:3 NIV

"With long life I will satisfy him and show him my salvation."

Psalm 91:16 ESV

Whoever finds me finds life, and obtains favor from the LORD.

Proverbs 8:35 NKJV

"Give ear and come to me; hear me, that your soul may live. I will make an everlasting covenant with you, my faithful love promised to David."

Isaiah 55:3 NIV

"Therefore I tell you, do not worry about your life, what you will eat or drink; or about your body, what you will wear. Is not life more important than food, and the body more important than clothes?"

Matthew 6:25 NIV

Jesus said to them, "I am the bread of life. He who comes to Me shall never hunger, and he who believes in Me shall never thirst."

John 6:35 NKJV

Miracles

Jesus did many other miraculous signs in the presence of the disciples, which are not recorded in this book. But these are written that you may believe that Jesus is the Christ, the Son of God.

John 20:30-31 NIV

In the New Testament Jesus performed various miracles: the feeding of the five thousand; cripples who walked and blind who saw. Which miracle do you find most amazing?

Your answer to this question may be personal. The Master may have healed you; your prayers may have been answered in a wonderful way; your life may have been changed irrevocably by the love of the Savior.

Could there ever be a greater miracle than the overwhelming fact that you have received new life in Jesus Christ? Jesus is the biggest miracle of all. He came to reveal the heavenly Father to people.

Jesus Christ is eternal and cannot be limited by time and space. He is the most awe-inspiring miracle of all time and is as real today as when He lived on earth.

God's Wondrous Deeds

You alone are the Lord. You made the heavens, even the highest heavens, and all their starry host, the earth and all that is on it, the seas and all that is in them. You give life to everything, and the multitudes of heaven worship you.

Nehemiah 9:6 NIV

You have multiplied, O Lord my God, your wondrous deeds and your thoughts toward us; none can compare with you! I will proclaim and tell of them, yet they are more than can be told.

Psalm 40:5 ESV

Jesus of Nazareth was a man accredited by God to you by miracles, wonders and signs, which God did among you through him, as you yourselves know.

Acts 2:22 NIV

He stilled the storm to a whisper; the waves of the sea were hushed. They were glad when it grew calm, and he guided them to their desired haven.

Psalm 107:29-30 NIV

"I will show wonders in heaven above and signs in the earth beneath."

Acts 2:19 NKJV

Taking the five loaves and the two fish and looking up to heaven, he gave thanks and broke the loaves. Then he gave them to his disciples to set before the people. He also divided the two fish among them all. The number of the men who had eaten was five thousand.

Mark 6:41, 44 NIV

He brought them out, after that he had shewed wonders and signs in the land of Egypt, and in the Red Sea, and in the wilderness forty years.

Acts 7:36 KJV

Jesus saith unto her, "Said I not unto thee, that, if thou wouldest believe, thou shouldest see the glory of God?"

John 11:40 KJV

When he came near the place where the road goes down the Mount of Olives, the whole crowd of disciples began joyfully to praise God in loud voices for all the miracles they had seen.

Luke 19:37 NIV

Miracles

When the Sabbath had come, He began to teach in the synagogue. And many hearing Him were astonished, saying, "Where did this Man get these things? And what wisdom is this which is given to Him, that such mighty works are performed by His hands!"

Mark 6:2 NKJV

Does he who supplies the Spirit to you and works miracles among you do so by works of the law, or by hearing with faith?

Galatians 3:5 ESV

This salvation, which was first announced by the Lord, was confirmed to us by those who heard him. God also testified to it by signs, wonders and various miracles, and gifts of the Holy Spirit distributed according to his will.

Hebrews 2:3-4 NIV

At evening, when the sun had set, they brought to Him all who were sick and those who were demon-possessed. And the whole city was gathered together at the door. Then He healed many who were sick with various diseases, and cast out many demons.

Mark 1:32-34 NKJV

Perseverance

"He who endures to the end shall be saved."
Matthew 24:13 NKJV

Not to see results from your efforts can be very depressing. If after much effort and perseverance you see no signs of success, you easily become discouraged and fall into despair. So many worthwhile tasks were never completed because people became discouraged.

A study of the spiritual giants in the Bible will reveal how they persevered against enormous odds to do the work that God called them to do. Regardless of setbacks, ridicule, resistance and suffering, they persevered with determination until the glory of God's purpose was revealed, sometimes only after their death.

There will be times when things will be difficult and you will be tempted to believe that your efforts are in vain. That is the time to trust God completely. Spend quiet time with Him and He will carry you through. Let faith triumph over your feelings and rest assured that, in God's perfect timing, your efforts will bear fruit.

Reward for Perseverance

Let us not become weary in doing good, for at the proper time we will reap a harvest if we do not give up.

Galatians 6:9 NIV

If we endure, we will also reign with him. If we disown him, he will also disown us; if we are faithless, he will remain faithful, for he cannot disown himself.

2 Timothy 2:12-13 NIV

The Lord will fulfill his purpose for me; your love, O Lord, endures forever – do not abandon the works of your hands.

Psalm 138:8 NIV

He will render to each one according to his works: to those who by patience in well-doing seek for glory and honor and immortality, he will give eternal life.

Romans 2:6-7 ESV

We have come to share in Christ if we hold firmly till the end the confidence we had at first.

Hebrews 3:14 NIV

Promises from God for Powerful Living

Strengthened with all might, according to his glorious power, unto all patience and longsuffering with joyfulness; giving thanks unto the Father, which hath made us meet to be partakers of the inheritance of the saints in light.

Colossians 1:11-12 KJV

If we hope for what we do not yet have, we wait for it patiently.

Romans 8:25 NIV

Blessed is the man that endureth temptation: for when he is tried, he shall receive the crown of life, which the Lord hath promised to them that love him.

James 1:12 KJV

Therefore, since we are surrounded by such a great cloud of witnesses, let us throw off everything that hinders and the sin that so easily entangles, and let us run with perseverance the race marked out for us.

Hebrews 12:1 NIV

More than that, we rejoice in our sufferings, knowing that suffering produces endurance, and endurance produces character, and character produces hope.

Romans 5:3-4 ESV

Perseverance

"The one who conquers will have this heritage, and I will be his God and he will be my son."

Revelation 21:7 ESV

Be still before the LORD and wait patiently for him; do not fret when men succeed in their ways, when they carry out their wicked schemes. Refrain from anger and turn from wrath; do not fret – it leads only to evil. For evil men will be cut off, but those who hope in the LORD will inherit the land.

Psalm 37:7-9 NIV

For you have need of endurance, so that after you have done the will of God, you may receive the promise.

Hebrews 10:36 NKJV

Consider it pure joy, my brothers, whenever you face trials of many kinds, because you know that the testing of your faith develops perseverance. Perseverance must finish its work so that you may be mature and complete, not lacking anything.

James 1:2-4 NIV

We rejoice in sufferings, because we know that suffering produces perseverance.

Romans 5:3 NIV

GROWTH

Therefore let us leave the elementary teachings about Christ and go on to maturity.

Hebrews 6:1 NIV

Unfortunately many Christians make little or no progress in their spiritual pilgrimage after getting to know Christ as their Savior. They claim to be Christians, but they have either forsaken their first love, or their faith has fallen into a rut.

To determine whether or not you are growing spiritually, ask yourself: has Christ become more and more real to you? Is prayer an essential part of your decision-making? Do you regard the Scriptures as the revelation of God's will for your life? Are you growing nearer to Christ every day?

It requires courage and honesty to answer these questions. Regardless of failures or the past, the Holy Spirit will inspire you to develop an awareness of Christ's presence. There is no end to spiritual growth and development, because the more you become aware of Christ's presence, the greater your love for Him becomes.

Bearing Fruit
for the Kingdom

They will be called oaks of righteousness, a planting of the Lord for the display of his splendor.

Isaiah 61:3 NIV

For every one that useth milk is unskilful in the word of righteousness: for he is a babe. But strong meat belongeth to them that are of full age, even those who by reason of use have their senses exercised to discern both good and evil.

Hebrews 5:13-14 KJV

As newborn babes, desire the pure milk of the word, that you may grow thereby, if indeed you have tasted that the Lord is gracious.

1 Peter 2:2-3 NKJV

All scripture is given by inspiration of God, and is profitable for doctrine, for reproof, for correction, for instruction in righteousness: That the man of God may be perfect, thoroughly furnished unto all good works.

2 Timothy 3:16-17 KJV

Promises from God for Powerful Living

Blessed is the man that walketh not in the counsel of the ungodly, nor standeth in the way of sinners, nor sitteth in the seat of the scornful. But his delight is in the law of the Lord; and in his law doth he meditate day and night. And he shall be like a tree planted by the rivers of water, that bringeth forth his fruit in his season; his leaf also shall not wither; and whatsoever he doeth shall prosper.

Psalm 1:1-3 KJV

"I am the vine; you are the branches. If a man remains in me and I in him, he will bear much fruit; apart from me you can do nothing. If anyone does not remain in me, he is like a branch that is thrown away and withers; such branches are picked up, thrown into the fire and burned. If you remain in me and my words remain in you, ask whatever you wish, and it will be given you. This is to my Father's glory, that you bear much fruit, showing yourselves to be my disciples."

John 15:5-8 NIV

It is my prayer that your love may abound more and more, with knowledge and all discernment.

Philippians 1:9 ESV

Growth

Then we will no longer be infants, tossed back and forth by the waves, and blown here and there by every wind of teaching and by the cunning and craftiness of men in their deceitful scheming. Instead, speaking the truth in love, we will in all things grow up into him who is the Head, that is, Christ.

Ephesians 4:14-15 NIV

We pray this in order that you may live a life worthy of the Lord and may please him in every way: bearing fruit in every good work, growing in the knowledge of God.

Colossians 1:10 NIV

We are bound to thank God always for you, brethren, as it is meet, because that your faith groweth exceedingly, and the charity of every one of you all toward each other aboundeth.

2 Thessalonians 1:3 KJV

Grow in the grace and knowledge of our Lord and Savior Jesus Christ. To Him be the glory both now and forever. Amen.

2 Peter 3:18 NKJV

Praise and Worship

Praise ye the Lord. O give thanks unto the Lord; for he is good: for his mercy endureth for ever.

Psalm 106:1 KJV

How much joy do you draw from your prayer life? When you pray today, make an effort to, "Sing for joy to God."

Open a hymn book, or put on a CD of worship music and use it to set the mood for a time of real praise and worship to God. Any celebration, however big or small, makes use of music. Music and singing are able to express the thoughts and feelings of the heart in a unique way.

That is why believers sing when they come together to worship God. In such times we remember how majestic God is, and the harmony of our singing tells the world how grateful we, His children, truly are. In Psalm 81, God's people are called to worship and praise: every song of praise is in itself a prayer! Sing songs of praise to God in your quiet time and experience new meaning in your life.

Glorifying God through Praise and Worship

I will extol the Lord at all times; his praise will always be on my lips.

Psalm 34:1 NIV

Bless the Lord, O my soul: and all that is within me, bless his holy name. Bless the Lord, O my soul, and forget not all his benefits.

Psalm 103:1-2 KJV

Make a joyful noise to the Lord, all the earth! Serve the Lord with gladness! Come into his presence with singing! Know that the Lord, he is God! It is he who made us, and we are his; we are his people, and the sheep of his pasture. Enter his gates with thanksgiving, and his courts with praise! Give thanks to him; bless his name!

Psalm 100:1-4 ESV

For as the earth bringeth forth her bud, and as the garden causeth the things that are sown in it to spring forth; so the Lord God will cause righteousness and praise to spring forth before all the nations.

Isaiah 61:11 KJV

Promises from God for Powerful Living

Therefore by Him let us continually offer the sacrifice of praise to God, that is, the fruit of our lips, giving thanks to His name.

Hebrews 13:15 NKJV

"Worthy is the Lamb that was slain to receive power, and riches, and wisdom, and strength, and honour, and glory, and blessing."

Revelation 5:12 KJV

Come, let us bow down in worship, let us kneel before the LORD our Maker.

Psalm 95:6 NIV

At the name of Jesus every knee should bow, of those in heaven, and of those on earth, and of those under the earth.

Philippians 2:10 NKJV

Worthy are you, our Lord and God, to receive glory and honor and power, for you created all things, and by your will they existed and were created.

Revelation 4:11 ESV

Praise the LORD! For it is good to sing praises to our God; for it is pleasant, and praise is beautiful.

Psalm 147:1 NKJV

Praise and Worship

You turned my wailing into dancing; you removed my sackcloth and clothed me with joy, that my heart may sing to you and not be silent. O Lord my God, I will give you thanks forever.

Psalm 30:11-12 NIV

It is good to give thanks to the Lord, to sing praises to your name, O Most High.

Psalm 92:1 ESV

Let everything that has breath praise the Lord. Praise the Lord.

Psalm 150:6 NIV

"But the hour cometh, and now is, when the true worshippers shall worship the Father in spirit and in truth: for the Father seeketh such to worship him. God is a Spirit: and they that worship him must worship him in spirit and in truth."

John 4:23-24 KJV

Praise be to the Lord God, the God of Israel, who alone does marvelous deeds. Praise be to his glorious name forever; may the whole earth be filled with his glory. Amen and Amen.

Psalm 72:18-19 NIV

Prayer

"If you remain in me and my words remain in you, ask whatever you wish, and it will be given you."

John 15:7 NIV

Some people maintain that prayer is easy while others believe it is difficult. If you are trying to develop a growing and meaningful prayer life, you will know that both these statements contain some truth.

With the best intentions in your heart you set aside time for prayer, but just as you begin, something intrudes upon these precious moments: a telephone call, a knock at the door, you suddenly remember something you should have done.

Pray about these things and change the disturbances into topics for prayer. Prayer is a dynamic, pulsating force that needs to be used continually if it is to retain its power and fulfill its function of leading you into a more intimate relationship with God. If your prayer life is weak it cannot fulfill the task for which it was created. Recharge your prayer batteries through disciplined prayer and see how God starts working in your life once more.

Powerful Prayer

"But when you pray, go into your room and shut the door and pray to your Father who is in secret. And your Father, who sees in secret will reward you."

Matthew 6:6 ESV

Pray continually.

1 Thessalonians 5:17 NIV

"Ask and it will be given to you; seek and you will find; knock and the door will be opened to you. For everyone who asks receives; he who seeks finds; and to him who knocks, the door will be opened."

Matthew 7:7-8 NIV

"Whatsoever ye shall ask in my name, that will I do, that the Father may be glorified in the Son."

John 14:13 KJV

The Lord is near to all who call on him, to all who call on him in truth. He fulfills the desires of those who fear him; he also hears their cry and saves them.

Psalm 145:18-19 ESV

Promises from God for Powerful Living

Beloved, if our heart does not condemn us, we have confidence toward God. And whatever we ask we receive from Him, because we keep His commandments and do those things that are pleasing in His sight.

1 John 3:21-22 NKJV

This is the confidence that we have in him, that, if we ask any thing according to his will, he heareth us: And if we know that he hear us, whatsoever we ask, we know that we have the petitions that we desired of him.

1 John 5:14-15 KJV

Do not be anxious about anything, but in everything, by prayer and petition, with thanksgiving, present your requests to God.

Philippians 4:6 NIV

O Lord, in the morning you hear my voice; in the morning I prepare a sacrifice for you and watch.

Psalm 5:3 ESV

Hear my prayer, O Lord, give ear to my supplications! In Your faithfulness answer me, and in Your righteousness.

Psalm 143:1 NKJV

Prayer

The righteous cry out, and the LORD hears them; he delivers them from all their troubles.

> Psalm 34:17 NIV

"It shall come to pass, that before they call, I will answer; and while they are yet speaking, I will hear."

> Isaiah 65:24 KJV

Let us then approach the throne of grace with confidence, so that we may receive mercy and find grace to help us in our time of need.

> Hebrews 4:16 NIV

He spake a parable unto them to this end, that men ought always to pray, and not to faint.

> Luke 18:1 KJV

"Have faith in God," Jesus answered. "I tell you the truth, if anyone says to this mountain, 'Go, throw yourself into the sea,' and does not doubt in his heart but believes that what he says will happen, it will be done for him. Therefore I tell you, whatever you ask for in prayer, believe that you have received it, and it will be yours."

> Mark 11:22-24 NIV

Priorities

"Seek first his kingdom and his righteousness, and all these things will be given to you as well."

Matthew 6:33 NIV

Many of God's servants are so busy working for Him that they do not find time to have regular quiet times. Service without prayer tends to become meaningless. The truth is that they are so active for the kingdom that gradually their activities become more important than their quiet time. They are working for God without experiencing the presence and power of the living Christ.

If the vision of what you are doing for the Lord fades, your service will become powerless and ineffective. This will happen because your spiritual reserves are not regularly replenished through prayer and meditation. Furthermore, you cannot be an effective witness for Christ without the power of prayer.

Put the Master foremost in all your activities, your service must be the result of your intimate relationship with Him. Only when He enjoys priority in all things, can you understand life the way He sees it.

God-centered Priorities

"So do not worry, saying, 'What shall we eat?' or 'What shall we drink?' or 'What shall we wear?' For the pagans run after all these things, and your heavenly Father knows that you need them. But seek first his kingdom and his righteousness, and all these things will be given to you as well."

Matthew 6:31-33 NIV

The Lord answered her, "Martha, Martha, you are anxious and troubled about many things, but one thing is necessary. Mary has chosen the good portion, which will not be taken away from her."

Luke 10:41-42 ESV

One thing I have desired of the LORD, that will I seek: That I may dwell in the house of the LORD all the days of my life, to behold the beauty of the LORD, and to inquire in His temple.

Psalm 27:4 NKJV

Do not be slothful in zeal, be fervent in spirit, serve the Lord.

Romans 12:11 ESV

Promises from God for Powerful Living

He said to them all, "If any man will come after me, let him deny himself, and take up his cross daily, and follow me. For whosoever will save his life shall lose it: but whosoever will lose his life for my sake, the same shall save it. For what is a man advantaged, if he gain the whole world, and lose himself, or be cast away?"

Luke 9:23-25 KJV

The fear of the LORD is the beginning of wisdom; all who practice it have a good understanding. His praise endures forever!

Psalm 111:10 ESV

"Therefore I tell you, do not worry about your life, what you will eat or drink; or about your body, what you will wear. Is not life more important than food, and the body more important than clothes?"

Matthew 6:25 NIV

Jesus said unto him, "No man, having put his hand to the plough, and looking back, is fit for the kingdom of God."

Luke 9:62 KJV

Fear the LORD your God, serve him only.

Deuteronomy 6:13 NIV

Priorities

He answering said, "Thou shalt love the Lord thy God with all thy heart, and with all thy soul, and with all thy strength, and with all thy mind; and thy neighbour as thyself."

Luke 10:27 KJV

"I tell you, whoever acknowledges me before men, the Son of Man will also acknowledge him before the angels of God."

Luke 12:8 NIV

The fear of the LORD is the beginning of wisdom; all who follow his precepts have good understanding. To him belongs eternal praise.

Psalm 111:10 NIV

Let not mercy and truth forsake thee: bind them about thy neck; write them upon the table of thine heart: So shalt thou find favour and good understanding in the sight of God and man.

Proverbs 3:3-4 KJV

Zeal for Your house has eaten me up, and the reproaches of those who reproach You have fallen on me.

Psalm 69:9 NKJV

Rest

He who dwells in the shelter of the Most High will rest in the shadow of the Almighty.

Psalm 91:1 NIV

People are desperately seeking peace and quiet from the stresses and strains of everyday life. Where do you find relief to carry on in the rat race we are caught up in?

There is only one way to cope with life and find peace. It is through unconditional commitment to Christ. He promised, "My peace I give you. I do not give to you as the world gives" (John 14:27 NIV).

Whatever problems you may be experiencing, no matter how serious, open your heart to the compassionate love of Jesus Christ. Allow Him to take complete control of your life. Spend time meditating on His Word, sitting at His feet in love and adoration. Make Him your constant Companion and pray without ceasing.

Then, when the storms in your life have subsided and your spirit once again experiences peace, you will know that you have found the peace of God that passes all understanding.

Peace and Perfect Rest in God

"Come to me, all you who are weary and burdened, and I will give you rest. Take my yoke upon you and learn from me, for I am gentle and humble in heart, and you will find rest for your souls."

Matthew 11:28-29 NIV

For thus saith the Lord God, the Holy One of Israel; In returning and rest shall ye be saved; in quietness and in confidence shall be your strength: and ye would not.

Isaiah 30:15 KJV

You will feel secure, because there is hope; you will look around and take your rest in security.

Job 11:18 ESV

He will not let your foot be moved; he who keeps you will not slumber. Behold, he who keeps Israel will neither slumber nor sleep.

Psalm 121:3-4 ESV

He grants sleep to those he loves.

Psalm 127:2 NIV

Truly my soul silently waits for God; from Him comes my salvation.

Psalm 62:1 NKJV

Return, O my soul, to your rest; for the LORD has dealt bountifully with you.

Psalm 116:7 ESV

The fear of the LORD tendeth to life: and he that hath it shall abide satisfied; he shall not be visited with evil.

Proverbs 19:23 KJV

"The beloved of the LORD shall dwell in safety by Him, who shelters him all the day long; and he shall dwell between His shoulders."

Deuteronomy 33:12 NKJV

For with stammering lips and another tongue will he speak to this people. To whom he said, "This is the rest wherewith ye may cause the weary to rest; and this is the refreshing: yet they would not hear."

Isaiah 28:11-12 KJV

They rested on the Sabbath in obedience to the commandment.

Luke 23:56 NIV

Rest

There remains, then, a Sabbath-rest for the people of God; for anyone who enters God's rest also rests from his own work, just as God did from his. Let us, therefore, make every effort to enter that rest, so that no one will fall by following their example of disobedience.

Hebrews 4:9-11 NIV

I will lie down and sleep in peace, for you alone, O LORD, make me dwell in safety.

Psalm 4:8 NIV

Find rest, O my soul, in God alone; my hope comes from him.

Psalm 62:5 NIV

My heart is glad and my tongue rejoices; my body will rest secure.

Psalm 16:9 NIV

When thou liest down, thou shalt not be afraid: yea, thou shalt lie down, and thy sleep shall be sweet.

Proverbs 3:24 KJV

Self-worth

*Know that the L*ORD*, he is God! It is he who made us, and we are his; we are his people, and the sheep of his pasture.*

Psalm 100:3 ESV

It is a sad fact that many people struggle to understand themselves. They spend long and agonizing hours in self-examination; they study psychology or visit psychologists to arrive at a better and more profound understanding of their personalities.

Unfortunately psychological self-examination can lead to self-centeredness, which in turn results in frustration and dissatisfaction.

In order to understand yourself, you have to accept and appreciate the fact that God created you in His image. This realization will bring you into harmony with yourself.

If Christ Jesus is Lord of your life and if you give Him priority over everything else in your life, your personal life will begin to acquire meaning and purpose. Consequently you will also experience the fulfillment of getting to know and value your true self.

Your Worth in Christ

Then God said, "Let us make man in our image, in our likeness, and let them rule over the fish of the sea and the birds of the air, over the livestock, over all the earth, and over all the creatures that move along the ground."

Genesis 1:26 NIV

"Are not two sparrows sold for a penny? Yet not one of them will fall to the ground apart from the will of your Father. And even the very hairs of your head are all numbered. So don't be afraid; you are worth more than many sparrows."

Matthew 10:29-31 NIV

Keep me as the apple of the eye, hide me under the shadow of thy wings.

Psalm 17:8 KJV

What, then, shall we say in response to this? If God is for us, who can be against us? He who did not spare his own Son, but gave him up for us all – how will he not also, along with him, graciously give us all things?

Romans 8:31-32 NIV

Promises from God for Powerful Living

God demonstrates His own love toward us, in that while we were still sinners, Christ died for us.

Romans 5:8 NKJV

Behold, what manner of love the Father hath bestowed upon us, that we should be called the sons of God: therefore the world knoweth us not, because it knew him not.

1 John 3:1 KJV

Let nothing be done through strife or vainglory; but in lowliness of mind let each esteem other better than themselves. Look not every man on his own things, but every man also on the things of others.

Philippians 2:3-4 KJV

As it is, God arranged the members in the body, each one of them, as he chose. If all were a single member, where would the body be? As it is, there are many parts, yet one body.

1 Corinthians 12:18-20 ESV

The LORD hath appeared of old unto me, saying, "Yea, I have loved thee with an everlasting love: therefore with lovingkindness have I drawn thee."

Jeremiah 31:3 KJV

Self-worth

You are a chosen people, a royal priesthood, a holy nation, a people belonging to God, that you may declare the praises of him who called you out of darkness into his wonderful light.

1 Peter 2:9 NIV

He chose us in Him before the foundation of the world, that we should be holy and without blame before Him in love, having predestined us to adoption as sons by Jesus Christ to Himself, according to the good pleasure of His will, to the praise of the glory of His grace, by which He made us accepted in the Beloved.

Ephesians 1:4-6 NKJV

God willed to make known what are the riches of the glory of this mystery among the Gentiles: which is Christ in you, the hope of glory.

Colossians 1:27 NKJV

For you created my inmost being; you knit me together in my mother's womb. I praise you because I am fearfully and wonderfully made; your works are wonderful, I know that full well.

Psalm 139:13-14 NIV

STRENGTH

I can do all things through him who strengthens me.
Philippians 4:13 ESV

Sometimes things get too much for us to handle and we feel as if we cannot move one step forward. If this is how you are feeling right now, the Lord wants to encourage you through His words, "Be of good courage, and He shall strengthen thine heart" (Ps. 27:14 KJV).

In the dark hours of his life David made the following discovery, "The LORD is the strength of my life" (Ps. 27:1 KJV). Even though the sun sometimes sets over your life, you never need dwell in darkness. With the Lord there is always light; He makes the night disappear.

Even though you feel hopelessly ensnared in your crises, the Lord will save you from all your distress and anxiety, even though you don't know when and how.

The Lord is your refuge where you will find protection, safety and rest. May the Lord carry you in love with this encouragement.

Renewed Strength
for Every Day

Those who hope in the Lord will renew their strength. They will soar on wings like eagles; they will run and not grow weary, they will walk and not be faint.

Isaiah 40:31 NIV

But ye shall receive power, after that the Holy Ghost is come upon you: and ye shall be witnesses unto me both in Jerusalem, and in all Judaea, and in Samaria, and unto the uttermost part of the earth.

Acts 1:8 KJV

God has incomparably great power for us who believe. That power is like the working of his mighty strength, which he exerted in Christ when he raised him from the dead and seated him at his right hand in the heavenly realms.

Ephesians 1:19-20 NIV

I want to know Christ and the power of his resurrection and the fellowship of sharing in his sufferings, becoming like him in his death.

Philippians 3:10 NIV

Finally, my brethren, be strong in the Lord and in the power of His might.

Ephesians 6:10 NKJV

He said to me, "My grace is sufficient for you, for my power is made perfect in weakness." Therefore I will boast all the more gladly about my weaknesses, so that Christ's power may rest on me. That is why, for Christ's sake, I delight in weaknesses, in insults, in hardships, in persecutions, in difficulties. For when I am weak, then I am strong.

2 Corinthians 12:9-10 NIV

The LORD is my strength and my song; he has become my salvation. He is my God, and I will praise him, my father's God, and I will exalt him.

Exodus 15:2 NIV

We have this treasure in earthen vessels, that the excellency of the power may be of God, and not of us.

2 Corinthians 4:7 KJV

My flesh and my heart faileth: but God is the strength of my heart, and my portion for ever.

Psalm 73:26 KJV

Strength

God is our refuge and strength, a very present help in trouble.

Psalm 46:1 ESV

The LORD is my strength and my shield; my heart trusted in Him, and I am helped; therefore my heart greatly rejoices, and with my song I will praise Him.

Psalm 28:7 NKJV

The name of the LORD is a strong tower; the righteous run to it and are safe.

Proverbs 18:10 NKJV

We pray this in order that you may live a life worthy of the Lord and may please him in every way: bearing fruit in every good work, growing in the knowledge of God, being strengthened with all power according to his glorious might so that you may have great endurance and patience.

Colossians 1:10-11 NIV

The LORD is their strength, and he is the saving strength of his anointed.

Psalm 28:8 NIV

He gives strength to the weary and increases the power of the weak.

Isaiah 40:29 NIV

SUCCESS

Has not God chosen those who are poor in the eyes of the world to be rich in faith and to inherit the kingdom he promised those who love him?

James 2:5 NIV

If we say that God's way leads to success, cynics might declare that the Christian message is too idealistic to be of any practical value in striving for success.

Christ showed the way of love through His death. He emphasized the great demands of such a path and He proved that even in death, love could triumph.

Although many people reject the way of Christian love, they have nothing to replace it. They propose political and social systems as solutions for the world's problems, but God's path is the only road to success.

God did not call humankind to an unattainable ideal in order to achieve success. However, His way requires sacrifice and those who risk putting it into practice will discover that it is the only path to true success.

What the Word says about Success

What good will it be for a man if he gains the whole world, yet forfeits his soul? Or what can a man give in exchange for his soul?

Matthew 16:26 NIV

Commit to the Lord whatever you do and your plans will succeed.

Proverbs 16:3 NIV

Everyone also to whom God has given wealth and possessions and power to enjoy them, and to accept his lot and rejoice in his toil – this is the gift of God.

Ecclesiastes 5:19 ESV

Blessed is every one that feareth the Lord; that walketh in his ways. For thou shalt eat the labour of thine hands: happy shalt thou be, and it shall be well with thee.

Psalm 128:1-2 KJV

If they obey and serve him, they shall spend their days in prosperity, and their years in pleasures.

Job 36:11 KJV

Command those who are rich in this present age not to be haughty, nor to trust in uncertain riches but in the living God, who gives us richly all things to enjoy.

1 Timothy 6:17 NKJV

His divine power has given us everything we need for life and godliness through our knowledge of him who called us by his own glory and goodness. Through these he has given us his very great and precious promises, so that through them you may participate in the divine nature and escape the corruption in the world caused by evil desires.

2 Peter 1:3-4 NIV

The LORD was with Joseph and gave him success in whatever he did.

Genesis 39:23 NIV

"Be strong and very courageous. Be careful to obey all the law my servant Moses gave you; do not turn from it to the right or to the left, that you may be successful wherever you go. Do not let this Book of the Law depart from your mouth; meditate on it day and night, so that you may be careful to do everything written in it. Then you will be prosperous and successful."

Joshua 1:7-8 NIV

Success

Hearken, my beloved brethren, hath not God chosen the poor of this world rich in faith, and heirs of the kingdom which he hath promised to them that love him?

James 2:5 KJV

David had success in all his undertakings, for the Lord was with him.

1 Samuel 18:14 ESV

Blessed is the man who does not walk in the counsel of the wicked or stand in the way of sinners or sit in the seat of mockers. But his delight is in the law of the Lord, and on his law he meditates day and night. He is like a tree planted by streams of water, which yields its fruit in season and whose leaf does not wither. Whatever he does prospers.

Psalm 1:1-3 NIV

Observe and obey all these words which I command you, that it may go well with you and your children after you forever, when you do what is good and right in the sight of the Lord your God.

Deuteronomy 12:28 NKJV

Thankfulness

Give thanks in all circumstances, for this is God's will for you in Christ Jesus.

1 Thessalonians 5:18 NIV

You do not have to look very far to find something to complain about. However, a wise person always tries to restore the balance by thinking about something to be grateful for. Remember, for everything that causes sorrow, there is something for which you can be eternally grateful.

If you have developed a grateful heart, you have discovered one of the great secrets of a powerful life. Your personality will begin to take on a wise and joyful bent. Try to find something that you can be grateful for and praise God for it. Incorporate this thought into your way of life, so that your general attitude becomes one of grateful praise to God.

Look for His involvement in every sphere of your life. If you do that, you will experience an inner change and it will seem as if all the powers of goodwill are competing to be revealed through you.

A Grateful Heart

Give thanks to the Lord, for he is good. His love endures forever.

Psalm 136:1 NIV

Thanks be to God! He gives us the victory through our Lord Jesus Christ.

1 Corinthians 15:57 NIV

Be careful for nothing; but in every thing by prayer and supplication with thanksgiving let your requests be made known unto God.

Philippians 4:6 KJV

We give thanks to you, O God; we give thanks, for your name is near. We recount your wondrous deeds.

Psalm 75:1 ESV

Let the peace of Christ rule in your hearts, since as members of one body you were called to peace. And be thankful. Let the word of Christ dwell in you richly as you teach and admonish one another with all wisdom, and as you sing psalms, hymns and spiritual songs with gratitude in your hearts to God.

Colossians 3:15-16 NIV

Enter into His gates with thanksgiving, and into His courts with praise. Be thankful to Him, and bless His name. For the Lord is good; His mercy is everlasting.

Psalm 100:4-5 NKJV

Strengthened with all might, according to his glorious power, unto all patience and longsuffering with joyfulness; giving thanks unto the Father, which hath made us meet to be partakers of the inheritance of the saints in light.

Colossians 1:11-12 KJV

Oh come, let us sing to the Lord! Let us shout joyfully to the Rock of our salvation. Let us come before His presence with thanksgiving; Let us shout joyfully to Him with psalms.

Psalm 95:1-2 NKJV

How can we thank God enough for you in return for all the joy we have in the presence of our God because of you?

1 Thessalonians 3:9 NIV

The Lord is my strength and my shield; in him my heart trusts, and I am helped; my heart exults, and with my song I give thanks to him.

Psalm 28:7 ESV

Thankfulness

Is any one of you in trouble? He should pray. Is anyone happy? Let him sing songs of praise.

James 5:13 NIV

Blessing, and glory, and wisdom, and thanksgiving, and honour, and power, and might, be unto our God for ever and ever. Amen.

Revelation 7:12 KJV

Thanks be to God, who gives us the victory through our Lord Jesus Christ.

1 Corinthians 15:57 NKJV

Always giving thanks to God the Father for everything, in the name of our Lord Jesus Christ.

Ephesians 5:20 NIV

I will give to the Lord the thanks due to his righteousness, and I will sing praise to the name of the Lord, the Most High.

Psalm 7:17 ESV

And they were to stand every morning, thanking and praising the LORD, and likewise at evening.

1 Chronicles 23:30 ESV

Time

He said to them, "It is not for you to know times or seasons that the Father has fixed by his own authority."
Acts 1:7 ESV

All of us make plans and dream about our future at some time or another. In some cases these plans never materialize and remain dreams. When thorough planning has been done, however, dreams are often fulfilled. It was a wise man who noted that "he who fails to plan, plans to fail."

People who put their future in the hand of either "fate" or "Lady Luck" find their future clouded with insecurity. In the life of the Christian however; there is no such thing as fate. God is always in control! Therefore there's only one way you can work confidently on your future and that is by committing your whole life to Him.

Trust God unconditionally and wait on Him. In His perfect timing He will lead you into the future that He has planned for you. Enter the future with your hand in His.

God's Perfect Timing

To every thing there is a season, and a time to every purpose under the heaven.

Ecclesiastes 3:1 KJV

Jesus answered, "Are there not twelve hours of daylight? A man who walks by day will not stumble, for he sees by this world's light."

John 11:9 NIV

For He says, "In an acceptable time I have heard you, and in the day of salvation I have helped you." Behold, now is the accepted time; behold, now is the day of salvation.

2 Corinthians 6:2 NKJV

Walk as wise redeeming the time, because the days are evil.

Ephesians 5:16 KJV

Conduct yourselves wisely toward outsiders, making the best use of the time.

Colossians 4:5 ESV

Promises from God for Powerful Living

But, beloved, be not ignorant of this one thing, that one day is with the Lord as a thousand years, and a thousand years as one day.

2 Peter 3:8 KJV

Declaring the end from the beginning, and from ancient times things that are not yet done, saying, "My counsel shall stand, and I will do all My pleasure."

Isaiah 46:10 NKJV

In the beginning God created the heavens and the earth.

Genesis 1:1 NIV

"Therefore do not worry about tomorrow, for tomorrow will worry about itself. Each day has enough trouble of its own."

Matthew 6:34 NIV

When I saw him, I fell at his feet as though dead. But he laid his right hand on me, saying, "Fear not, I am the first and the last."

Revelation 1:17 ESV

"I will bless them. I will send down showers in season; there will be showers of blessing."

Ezekiel 34:26 NIV

Ye are all the children of light, and the children of the day: we are not of the night, nor of darkness.

1 Thessalonians 5:5 KJV

My voice You shall hear in the morning, O LORD; in the morning I will direct it to You, and I will look up.

Psalm 5:3 NKJV

Evening and morning and at noon I utter my complaint and moan, and he hears my voice.

Psalm 55:17 ESV

This is the day the LORD has made; let us rejoice and be glad in it.

Psalm 118:24 ESV

He has made everything beautiful in its time. He has also set eternity in the hearts of men; yet they cannot fathom what God has done from beginning to end.

Ecclesiastes 3:11 NIV

"I will send you rain in its season, and the ground will yield its crops."

Leviticus 26:4 NIV

WISDOM

For wisdom is more precious than rubies, and nothing you desire can compare with her.

Proverbs 8:11 NIV

It is possible to be highly educated while lacking spiritual insight. For the Christian, sanctification must always receive priority over education. This is a comforting truth for the child of God who, for whatever reason, has been denied a good education.

You may be disappointed about not having received a good education and feel inferior because you perceive others to be cleverer than you are. A person who is developing spiritually, is close to the heart of God and, therefore, skilled in understanding God's ways.

A spiritual person has discovered the true Source of wisdom in life. He possesses peace and inner strength born from fellowship with the Holy Spirit. Make time to get together with God. Put your requests before Him and allow the presence of God to penetrate your life so that you can serve Him in truth and so that His wisdom, peace and strength can flow through you.

Wise Words from the Word

The fear of the Lord is the beginning of wisdom; all who practice it have a good understanding. His praise endures forever!

Psalm 111:10 esv

Blessed is the man who finds wisdom, the man who gains understanding, for she is more profitable than silver and yields better returns than gold. She is more precious than rubies; nothing you desire can compare with her. Long life is in her right hand; in her left hand are riches and honor. Her ways are pleasant ways, and all her paths are peace. She is a tree of life to those who embrace her; those who lay hold of her will be blessed.

Proverbs 3:13-18 niv

"Therefore everyone who hears these words of mine and puts them into practice is like a wise man who built his house on the rock."

Matthew 7:24 niv

O the depth of the riches both of the wisdom and knowledge of God! How unsearchable are his judgments.

Romans 11:33 kjv

Promises from God for Powerful Living

If any of you lacks wisdom, let him ask God, who gives generously to all without reproach, and it will be given him.

James 1:5 ESV

The wisdom from above is first pure, then peaceable, gentle, open to reason, full of mercy and good fruits, impartial and sincere.

James 3:17 ESV

Wisdom and knowledge shall be the stability of thy times, and strength of salvation: the fear of the Lord is his treasure.

Isaiah 33:6 KJV

The law of the Lord is perfect, reviving the soul. The statutes of the Lord are trustworthy, making wise the simple. The precepts of the Lord are right, giving joy to the heart. The commands of the Lord are radiant, giving light to the eyes.

Psalm 19:7-8 NIV

For the Lord giveth wisdom: out of his mouth cometh knowledge and understanding. He layeth up sound wisdom for the righteous: he is a buckler to them that walk uprightly.

Proverbs 2:6-7 KJV

Wisdom

With God are wisdom and might; he has counsel and understanding.

Job 12:13 ESV

Thou through thy commandments hast made me wiser than mine enemies: for they are ever with me. I have more understanding than all my teachers: for thy testimonies are my meditation.

Psalm 119:98-99 KJV

Do not be wise in your own eyes; fear the LORD and depart from evil. It will be health to your flesh, and strength to your bones.

Proverbs 3:7-8 NKJV

Let the word of Christ dwell in you richly in all wisdom; teaching and admonishing one another in psalms and hymns and spiritual songs, singing with grace in your hearts to the Lord.

Colossians 3:16 KJV

WOMANHOOD

She dresses herself with strength and makes her arms strong.

Proverbs 31:17 ESV

Throughout the Scriptures women played an important role and their influence on the kingdom of God should not be underestimated. They were the last ones present at Jesus' cross and the first at His tomb. While Jesus ministered He was served by a group of women who used their own possessions to support Him and His disciples.

The church is greatly indebted to devout women who love Christ so much that they are willing to sacrifice everything. Many men are where they are today only because of the prayers and support of a loving wife or mother.

Paul tells us that there are no differences between men and women, Jews and Gentiles, slaves and free people: in Jesus Christ we are all one. This unity in Christ makes Christians dependent on one another. Therefore we should show respect and appreciation for the service that every person offers.

WISE WORDS FOR WOMEN

So the LORD God caused the man to fall into a deep sleep; and while he was sleeping, he took one of the man's ribs and closed up the place with flesh. Then the LORD God made a woman from the rib he had taken out of the man, and he brought her to the man. The man said, "This is now bone of my bones and flesh of my flesh; she shall be called 'woman', for she was taken out of man." For this reason a man will leave his father and mother and be united to his wife, and they will become one flesh. The man and his wife were both naked, and they felt no shame.

Genesis 2:21-25 NIV

In the Lord, however, woman is not independent of man, nor is man independent of woman. For as woman came from man, so also man is born of woman. But everything comes from God.

1 Corinthians 11:11-12 NIV

The wisest of women builds her house, but folly with her own hands tears it down.

Proverbs 14:1 ESV

Then the Lord God said, "It is not good that the man should be alone; I will make him a helper fit for him."

Genesis 2:18 ESV

"For this cause shall a man leave father and mother, and shall cleave to his wife: and they twain shall be one flesh? Wherefore they are no more twain, but one flesh. What therefore God hath joined together, let not man put asunder."

Matthew 19:5-6 KJV

Nevertheless let each one of you in particular so love his own wife as himself, and let the wife see that she respects her husband.

Ephesians 5:33 NKJV

Likewise, teach the older women to be reverent in the way they live, not to be slanderers or addicted to much wine, but to teach what is good. Then they can train the younger women to love their husbands and children, to be self-controlled and pure, to be busy at home, to be kind, and to be subject to their husbands, so that no one will malign the word of God.

Titus 2:3-5 NIV

Womanhood

For this is the way the holy women of the past who put their hope in God used to make themselves beautiful. They were submissive to their own husbands, like Sarah, who obeyed Abraham and called him her master. You are her daughters if you do what is right and do not give way to fear.

1 Peter 3:5-6 NIV

An excellent wife is the crown of her husband, but she who brings shame is like rottenness in his bones.

Proverbs 12:4 ESV

He who finds a wife finds a good thing and obtains favor from the Lord.

Proverbs 18:22 ESV

Her children arise and call her blessed; her husband also, and he praises her: "Many women do noble things, but you surpass them all." Charm is deceptive, and beauty is fleeting; but a woman who fears the Lord is to be praised.

Proverbs 31:28-30 NIV

Work

Commit your work to the Lord, and your plans will be established.

Proverbs 16:3 ESV

You must utilize the special talents and gifts that God has entrusted you with in your chosen profession. Do this so that you can do your share, regardless of how elementary or routine it may be.

All surgeons are dependent on the theater staff and they are essential to the success of every operation, especially those who have the humble task of attending to the hygiene of the operating theater. The success of a world-famous pianist would be impossible without the painfully conscientious attention of the piano tuner to his task.

Whatever task you are called to perform, do not neglect to thank God that He has chosen you to do it. Dedicate everything you do to Him and ask the Holy Spirit to guide you so that you will find perfect joy in the knowledge that you are doing it well because you are doing it to the glorification of your Master.

What the Word says about Work

The Lord God took the man, and put him into the garden of Eden to dress it and to keep it.

Genesis 2:15 KJV

"Six days shalt thou labour, and do all thy work: But the seventh day is the sabbath of the Lord thy God: in it thou shalt not do any work, thou, nor thy son, nor thy daughter, thy manservant, nor thy maidservant, nor thy cattle, nor thy stranger that is within thy gates."

Exodus 20:9 KJV

Unless the Lord builds the house, its builders labor in vain. Unless the Lord watches over the city, the watchmen stand guard in vain.

Psalm 127:1 NIV

There is nothing better for a man, than that he should eat and drink, and that he should make his soul enjoy good in his labour. This also I saw, that it was from the hand of God.

Ecclesiastes 2:24 KJV

Promises from God for Powerful Living

Whatever your hand finds to do, do it with your might; for there is no work or device or knowledge or wisdom in the grave where you are going.

Ecclesiastes 9:10 NKJV

Slaves, obey your earthly masters with respect and fear, and with sincerity of heart, just as you would obey Christ. Obey them not only to win their favor when their eye is on you, but like slaves of Christ, doing the will of God from your heart. Serve wholeheartedly, as if you were serving the Lord, not men.

Ephesians 6:5-7 NIV

Whatever you do, whether in word or deed, do it all in the name of the Lord Jesus, giving thanks to God the Father through him.

Colossians 3:17 NIV

Moreover, when God gives any man wealth and possessions, and enables him to enjoy them, to accept his lot and be happy in his work – this is a gift of God.

Ecclesiastes 5:19 NIV

Work

For the scripture saith, "Thou shalt not muzzle the ox that treadeth out the corn. And, the labourer is worthy of his reward."

1 Timothy 5:18 KJV

In all toil there is profit, but mere talk tends only to poverty.

Proverbs 14:23 ESV

A man will be satisfied with good by the fruit of his mouth, and the recompense of a man's hands will be rendered to him.

Proverbs 12:14 NKJV

Do you see a man skilled in his work? He will serve before kings; he will not serve before obscure men.

Proverbs 22:29 NIV

So I commend the enjoyment of life, because nothing is better for a man under the sun than to eat and drink and be glad. Then joy will accompany him in his work all the days of the life God has given him under the sun.

Ecclesiastes 8:15 NIV

OTHER BOOKS IN THIS RANGE

PROMISES FROM GOD FOR
PURPOSEFUL LIVING

ISBN: 186920-536-7

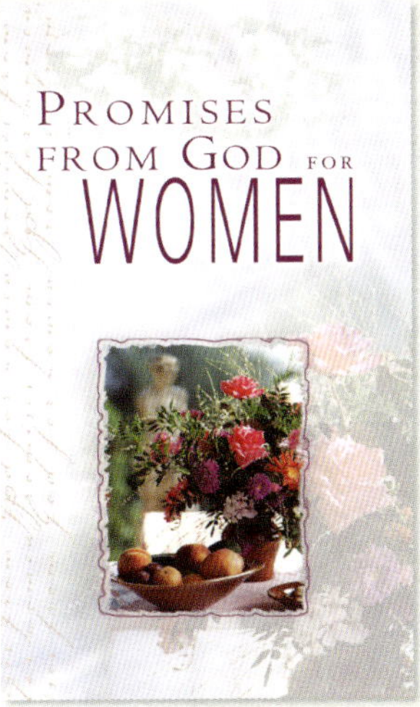

PROMISES FROM GOD FOR WOMEN

ISBN: 1-86920-070-5

PROMISES FROM GOD FOR TODAY

ISBN: 1-86920-069-1